KU-248-754

the
alphabet
book

**For my
children,
Joshua,
Lillie and
Edith**

First published in Great Britain
1999 by Aurum Press Ltd
25 Bedford Avenue, London WC1B 3AT

Copyright © Susie Johns 1999

Design by Ann Thomson

Photography by Debbie Patterson
Step-by-step photography by Lucy Mason
Additional photography by the author

All rights reserved. No part of this book may be reproduced or
utilized in any form or by any means, electronic or mechanical,
including photocopy, recording or by any information storage
and retrieval system, without written permission in writing from
Aurum Press Ltd.

The right of Susie Johns to be identified as author of this work
has been asserted by her in accordance with the Copyright,
Design and Patents Act 1988.

A catalogue record for this book is available from
the British Library.

ISBN 1 85410 616 3

10 9 8 7 6 5 4 3 2 1

2003 2002 2001 2000 1999

Printed in Hong Kong/China
by South China Printing Co. (1988) Ltd

the alphabet book

Alphabets for design and decoration

SUSIE JOHNS

AURUM PRESS

Contents

Introduction

From a very early age, the letters of the alphabet are recognizable to all of us. This book takes these familiar signs and uses them in all kinds of decorative ways. Whatever your existing craft skills, you will be able to recreate any or all of the projects set out on these pages – it's as easy as ABC!

Over twenty thousand years ago, humans made the first pictures, the remnants of which still exist in the caves of Lascaux, in France. About six thousand years ago, in Mesopotamia, the Sumerians made marks on clay tablets, to account for sacks of grain and sheep. The symbols used were simplified drawings, a system of accounting, but they are now considered to be the beginnings of written language.

It was the Phoenicians that invented the alphabet as such – symbols to correspond with spoken sounds – albeit one consisting only of consonants. Later, the Greeks added vowel sounds, and by about 500 BC, the Greek alphabet consisted of twenty-four letters: seventeen consonants and seven vowels, with both upper-case and lower-case versions of each letter.

ΛΠΑΒΟ

Letters have evolved over centuries to become as simple as possible, geometric in shape and form. Western alphabets have the fewest number of characters possible to convey, either individually or in combination, all our complex spoken sounds. But it is not as simple as that. The basic letter forms can be changed in style without altering their sounds or meaning. Each of us has his or her own style of handwriting, for example.

And graphic designers, the people who produce posters, packaging and typography for the pages of newspapers and magazines, play around with letter styles all the time.

The shapes, sizes and weights of the basic letters can be altered in all kinds of ways, frequently conveying different visual clues. Often we do not have to read every word of a poster or sign to understand what it is saying. The size, shape, colour or positioning of the letter shapes send out their own message. A copperplate script may denote a sense of history, formality and elegance; chunky, bright letters can seem childish or light-hearted; bold letters usually add weight and emphasis.

Lettering can convey moods: it can be serious, playful, threatening, spooky, romantic. It can convey to people, at a glance, all kinds of themes – Elizabethan, Gothic, Wild West, 1930s, Hollywood, Pop – and each of us will be attracted or repelled by different styles.

Alphabets are a vital system of written communication – but they are much more than this. In the modern urban world we are bombarded with a multitude of letter forms. Not only do letters convey messages, they are also decorative images in their own right. Advertisements, banners, neon signs, billboards, posters, shopfronts, signposts, commercial vehicles and graffiti all carry messages, some of which we read but all of which combine to make a decorative backdrop to city life. Though we may not consciously be aware of their meaning or even their presence, these messages are a constant source of visual stimulation.

The object of this book is to encourage the use of lettering in its many forms, as a decorative device. Whether you are stitching a quilt, redecorating a room or planning a party, there are lots of ways to use lettering as adornment.

You will find more than sixty ideas throughout the book, some of which are quick and easy to do, others requiring a bit more time, effort and skill. The projects are diverse, employing a range of techniques, but all are within the reach of most people.

Each project is illustrated with a colour photograph of the finished item, while the method of making it is described step-by-step. Some of the steps are illustrated, for extra clarity. You will also find suggestions for adapting and varying designs and templates so that, for example, an embroidered motif might instead be applied to a piece of furniture and

ANDAL MERCIABLE QUENE,

painted, or made into a greetings card. There is a library of designs at the back of the book, along with further descriptions of some of the techniques used

There is not enough room in a book of this size to give more than a few whole alphabets to use as templates, but you will find rich sources of material all around you, particularly in magazines. Search through the pages of most glossy monthlies and you will find, in both the advertising and editorial pages, lots of interesting typefaces that can be traced, photocopied, enlarged or reduced to make into monograms and messages. Children's illustrated storybooks, too, often feature interesting lettering. Or look at the packaging in your food cupboard for inspiration.

Use a camera to photograph interesting examples of lettering on billboards, on shopfronts or on the sides of vehicles. If you have access to a computer, you will have a selection of different typefaces at your disposal, and perhaps the means to manipulate letters, to make them smaller, taller, bolder, narrower, or reversed.

I have always had an interest in alphabets and letter forms. On my mother's side of the family, my great-grandfather's hobby was calligraphy, and he produced some lovely illuminated scripts *(opposite)*.

His son, my grandfather, wrote in a meticulous copperplate hand. When I was a child, my father was an illustrator on the local paper and all the wording he added, in captions, headings and advertisements, was hand-lettered *(above)*. As I learned to write, my father was concerned not only that my spelling and grammar should be accurate but that I should develop a graceful handwriting style, with elegant, well-proportioned letter shapes. His own handwriting is both stylish and completely legible.

At art school, I studied painting and printmaking and, not content with just pictorial images, I preferred to add words to convey my message. Now I earn my living as both a writer and editor, and a craftsperson working in fabric, thread and paper, and words and letters cross over into the objects I make. I find myself embroidering texts, printing letters on clothing and using alphabet letters to embellish all manner of things. I hope that readers of this book will find similar inspiration in alphabets.

Susie Johns

As easy as A B C

*A*lphabet letters perform a dual function in the nursery or playroom. Not only are they decorative but they can also help your child learn to read. Hand-painted or stencilled lettering can be applied to all kinds of things. Start by putting your child's name on the door. Then, what about labelling drawers with their contents – socks, shirts, shorts – or furniture with the appropriate names – chair, table, desk?

Toy Box & Cupboard

A plain wooden box can become home to a collection of special toys. This box is labelled 'circus' but could just as well say 'zoo' or 'farm' or any other favourite theme. Meanwhile, in a cupboard labelled 'ABC', a child could keep all sorts of things – but how about a whole alphabet of wooden capital letters?

You will need

Wooden box

Wooden cupboard

Fine-grade sandpaper

White gesso primer or emulsion paint

Acrylic paints in yellow, red and blue

Soft pencil (4B)

Carbon paper (optional)

Fine paintbrush

Acrylic varnish, satin finish

TIP You will find star shapes on page 114, as well as the template for 'circus'. If you'd prefer to use another word, try drawing it freehand on a piece of paper, making changes until you are satisfied with your design. Or trace letters from a magazine.

How to paint a toy box

1. Prepare the box. If wood is already painted or varnished, lightly sand the area to be decorated using fine-grade sandpaper. On raw wood, paint a base colour of white emulsion or gesso primer. Allow to dry.

2. Paint the whole box, inside and out, with yellow acrylic. You may prefer to paint the inside with red or blue, to provide a contrast. Leave to dry (about 2 hours).

3. Mark out two rectangles in pencil, one inside the other, to form a frame for the central image.

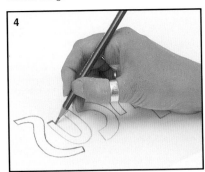

4. Trace the 'circus' template on page 114 on to tracing paper. Turn over and go over the lines on the reverse of the paper, using a soft pencil.

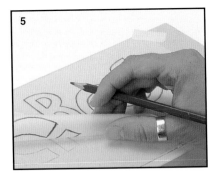

5. Place the paper, right side up, in position on the box. Hold it in place with a few strips of masking tape. Go over the letters again, to transfer them on to the painted surface. Add a border of stars.

6. Using a fine brush, fill in the letter and star shapes with acrylic paint. Do not overload the brush. Any mistakes can be wiped away using a damp cotton bud.

7. When the design is dry, paint over the whole area with two or three coats of acrylic varnish.

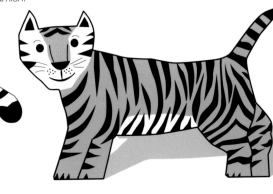

Wooden letters and animal shapes can be cut from plywood, using a jigsaw. Sand the edges, prime and paint.

TEMPLATES: Stars and Circus, page 114

Turn a plain wooden box into a travelling circus, to be filled with animal figures or perhaps some juggling balls?

A colourful
cupboard,
labelled
'ABC', could
contain wooden
alphabet letters
or bricks.

How to paint a cupboard

1. As with the box, if wood is already painted or varnished, lightly sand it in preparation.

2.. Paint the whole cupboard, inside and out, with white emulsion paint or primer. When dry, paint the outside of the cupboard, apart from the doors, yellow. Paint the doors white.

3. Stick strips of masking tape on the doors, then paint the gaps in between red. When paint is dry, remove the masking tape to reveal stripes.

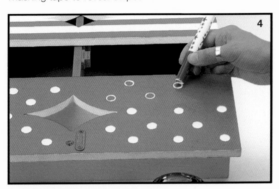

4. Paint the inside of the cupboard doors red. Leave to dry. To make the spots, dip a round object, such as the lid of a felt-tip pen, into white acrylic paint, and stamp spots in a regular pattern.

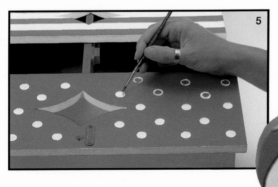

5. Fill in the spots, if necessary, with white paint applied with a fine brush.

6. When the paint is dry, protect your work with with two or three coats of acrylic varnish.

TEMPLATES: ABC, page 116

For a Little Girl...

A little chair, a stool, a flimsy nightdress, can be personalized with the name or initial of your own favourite little princess. If you have a steady, confident hand, you can draw the name freehand – using an eraser to correct mistakes – or you can trace the letters you need. Then paint, with easy-to-use acrylics, or stitch, to create your very own heirloom.

You will need

Fine sandpaper

Acrylic paints

Fine paintbrush

Acrylic varnish, satin finish

Make a tiny, herb-filled pillow to be hung from a ribbon loop above a child's bed. Copy this message or make up your own.

You will need

Pencil, erasable pen or transfer pen (see TIP)

6-stranded embroidery thread

How to paint a name

1. Prepare the furniture. If wood is already painted, lightly sand the area to be decorated, using a fine-grade sandpaper. On raw wood, paint a base colour of white emulsion. Then paint with a coat of acrylic. Allow to dry.

2. Draw letters freehand or trace, then transfer using carbon paper, or by tracing over the back of the design with a soft pencil.

3. Using a fine brush, fill in the letter shapes in your chosen colour. Do not overload the brush. Any mistakes can be wiped away using a damp cotton bud.

4. When the design is dry, sand lightly, particularly around the edges, for a distressed finish, then paint over the whole area with two or three coats of acrylic varnish, sanding lightly between coats.

How to stitch a name

1. Trace the lettering on to thin paper. If the fabric to be embroidered is quite sheer, place it over the design and trace directly on to the fabric, using a pencil or an erasable pen. If, however, the lines cannot be seen through the fabric, trace over the back of the design using a transfer pen. Place on the fabric and press with a hot iron, to transfer the design.

2. Stretch the area to be stitched in an embroidery hoop. With two strands of embroidery thread in your needle, fill in the letters using satin stitch for wider areas and stem stitch for thin lines.

3. Press the finished work lightly on the back.

4. To make the embroidered piece into a small cushion, follow the instructions on page 41.

TEMPLATES: Script Name, page 117

TECHNIQUES: Satin Stitch and Stem Stitch, page 113

TIP An ordinary pencil can be used to draw a design on fabric. The pencil lines will be covered by the embroidery stitches. You may, however, prefer to use a pen, as the design will show up better. Use a vanishing pen if the embroidery is to be completed quickly, as the lines will disappear within about 24 hours. If you intend to spend longer stitching, choose a water-erasable pen; when the embroidery is finished, the lines can be washed out or removed by dabbing with damp cotton wool.

A small stool can serve as a doll-sized table, with matching chair. The paint colours have been chosen to match the braid border on the small cushion. A lawn dress, purchased from an antique market, is personalized with a child's name.

Practical Pegs

A peg rack can be just a functional item: a place to hang your hat and coat. Or you can make a feature out of it, displaying a few well-chosen items. Either way, alphabet letters can provide the right enhancement. Stencilled initials help to identify which peg belongs to which family member. Or pegs could be labelled in an even more practical way: coat, hat, scarf, bag and so on. If you are using a peg rack to display some special articles, however, you may wish to be a bit more fanciful in your choice of lettering. A name, a quotation, a short line from a poem, or some beautifully wrought initials may be just the right thing to turn functional hangers into something much more decorative.

Children will love to have their own personalized peg – and lettering can be a simple or as intricate as your painting skills allow.

You will need

Wooden peg rack

Fine-grade sandpaper

White gesso primer or emulsion paint

Acrylic paints

Soft pencil (4B)

Carbon paper (optional)

Fine paintbrush

Acrylic varnish, satin finish

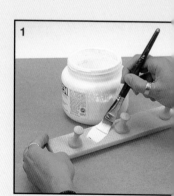

TIP Any functional piece of painted furniture, subject to a certain amount of wear and tear, needs the protection of several coats of varnish.

Painted initials can be used to allocate a separate peg to each family member.

How to paint a peg rack

1. Prepare the peg rack by lightly sanding, if necessary, to remove any varnish or paint, then cover with a coat of white emulsion or gesso primer. Allow to dry.

2. Paint the rack with a coat of acrylic in your chosen base colour. Leave to dry (about 2 hours).

3. Paint the pegs and any moulding in a contrasting colour. Leave to dry.

4. Mark out the lettering using a soft pencil, then, using a fine brush, fill in the letter shapes with acrylic paint.

5. A thick border line gives a neat finish. Steady your hand on the work surface and run the handle of the paintbrush along the edge of a ruler.

6. When the design is dry, paint over the whole area with two or three coats of acrylic varnish.

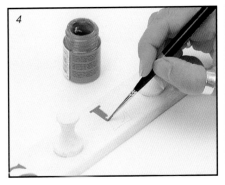

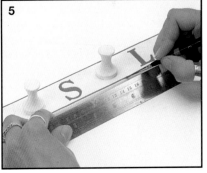

TEMPLATES: Alphabet, page 123

Appliqué Quilt

mall pieces of brightly coloured cotton fabric make a cheerful contemporary alphabet quilt and a personalized cushion cover.

The simple appliqué technique uses a sewing machine and iron-on bonding material for speed and accuracy. Letter shapes can be traced directly on to the bonding material and fused to the backing fabric using a hot iron.

Be brave in your choice of colours. In this example, no two squares use the same colour combinations. Shops selling patchwork fabrics offer a really wide range of colours, or you could dye plain white cotton, using fabric dyes.

You will need

Scraps of cotton fabric, at least 15 x 15 cm (6 x 6 in)

Bondaweb

95 x 69 cm (37¹/₂ x 27¹/₂ in) plain or printed cotton fabric, for backing

91 x 65 cm (35 x 25¹/₂ in) medium-weight wadding

Sewing thread, in various colours

How to make the quilt

1. Cut out thirty-five squares of fabric, each measuring 15 cm (6 in). Use lots of different colours. Arrange to form a grid, five squares by seven.

2. Stitch the squares together with a 1 cm (1/2 in) seam, in rows of five. Press seams open. Then join rows and press again.

3. Using the alphabet on page 120, enlarge the letters on a photocopier until they measure approximately 10 cm (4 in) tall. You will also need to reverse the letters (see TIP, page 27).

4. Trace each letter directly on to the paper backing of the Bondaweb. Cut out each one roughly, leaving a small margin all round.

5. Take small fabric scraps, each slightly larger than your chosen letter. Using a hot iron, following the manufacturer's directions, fuse the Bondaweb to the wrong side of the fabric.

6. Cut out each letter carefully, then peel off the paper backing. Place letters on the squares, positioning them centrally, then cover with a spare scrap of fabric, dampen slightly, and press with a hot iron for about 15 seconds, until firmly fused to the patchwork.

7. Using a contrasting coloured thread, stitch around each letter with a close zigzag stitch.

8. Cut out a piece of backing fabric 2.5 cm (1 in) larger all round than the quilt front. Place the two pieces together, with a layer of wadding sandwiched between. Pin and baste all layers, then quilt by stitching along seam lines.

9. To bind the edges of the quilt, fold under 1 cm (1/2 in) on the raw edge of the backing fabric, then fold over to cover the raw edge of the patchwork. Stitch in place by hand or machine, then press lightly.

Appliqué Cushion

How to make the cushion

1. Using the same method as for the quilt, fuse the letters of your choice on to a piece of plain coloured fabric. Stitch this to a larger piece of fabric, 1 cm (¹/₂ in) larger all round than your finished cushion.

2. One by one, place small scraps of fabric on the backing fabric and stitch in place using a medium zigzag stitch. There is no need to hem the pieces, or to turn raw edges under, as the zigzag stitch will prevent them from fraying too much. Alternatively, bond each piece in place, using Bondaweb.

3. When all the backing fabric is covered, add flower shapes (from page 114), using Bondaweb. Then stitch random lines of straight stitch all over the cover.

4. Cut a piece of plain or printed fabric the same size as the cushion front, to make the back of the cover. Stitch the two together, with right sides facing, 1 cm (¹/₂ in) from edges. Leave a gap on one side for turning. Clip corners and turn right sides out, insert cushion pad and slipstitch the opening closed.

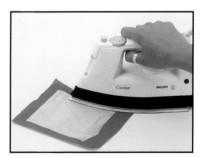

Once you have traced the letter, in reverse, on to the paper backing, fuse the Bondaweb to the wrong side of your fabric scrap.

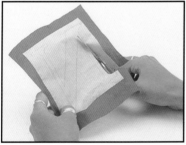

Carefully cut out the letter then peel off the paper backing. Lay the cutout letter in position, right side up, on the background fabric.

Press with a hot iron for approximately 15 seconds, to fuse the letter in place. You may find it easier to cover it with a damp cloth.

TIP Many modern photocopiers have the facility for reversing. If this is not available, tape the copy to a window, place the Bondaweb on top, and trace over the back of the copy.

TEMPLATES: Block Alphabet, page 120, Star and Flower, page 114

Rag Book

*T*his soft fabric book uses the same appliqué method used for the quilt on page 24. In other words, very little sewing is required, as fabric letters and shapes are bonded in place with the aid of a hot iron.

The effect is charming; the effort is minimal. If you are a beginner to the technique, why not start with a little picture? Once the bug has bitten, you can progress to a rag book for a baby. What lovelier way to introduce a child to the alphabet?

You will need

Scraps of cotton fabric
Bondaweb
Large eyelets and eyelet punch
Ribbon, 2.5 cm (1 in) wide

How to make a rag book

1. Cut out squares of fabric, each measuring 15 cm (6 in), two for each page.

2. Using the alphabet on page 121, trace your chosen letters on to tracing paper. Reverse the paper, and trace the letters on to the paper backing of the Bondaweb. Cut out each letter roughly, leaving a small margin all round.

3. Take small scraps of fabric, each slightly larger than your chosen letter. Using a hot iron, and following the manufacturer's directions,

fuse the Bondaweb on to the wrong side of the fabric.

4. Cut out each letter carefully, then peel off the paper backing. Place the letters, to spell simple words, on to the fabric squares. Cover with a spare scrap of fabric, dampen slightly, and press with a hot iron for about 15 seconds, until the letters are firmly fused to the backing fabric.

5. Add pictorial motifs, using the templates given, or adapting pictures from storybooks.

6. Place stitched pages together, right sides

facing. Place a piece of wadding on top. Stitch 1cm (1/2 in) from raw edges, round three sides. Clip corners; turn right sides out.

7. Turn raw edges to inside and slipstitch open side closed. Punch holes and insert eyelets. Use ribbons threaded through the eyelets, to attach the pages together.

TIP

Although you can use different types of fabric for appliqué, stick to 100 per cent cotton for the rag book, as it can easily be washed.

TEMPLATES: Block Alphabet, page 121, Animal Shapes, page 116

rag book is a colourful, enjoyable way to learn your ABC.

You will need

Medium-weight cotton fabric

Lengths of coloured ribbon

Matching sewing thread

40 cm (16 in) of cord, for drawstring

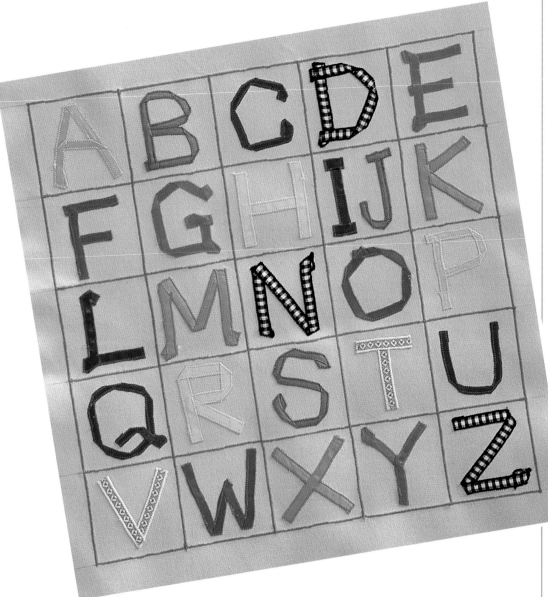

Use this alphabet as a reference when forming ribbon letters, or experiment with lengths of ribbon to form your own letter styles.

How to make a shoe bag

1. For the back and front of the bag cut two rectangles of fabric, each measuring 33 x 48 cm (13 x 19 in).

2. On the front piece, pin and stitch a length of ribbon across the width of the fabric, about 7.5 cm (3 in) from the bottom edge.

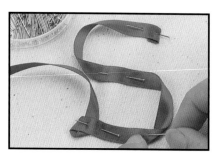

3. Using the widthways strip of ribbon as a guide to keep your letters straight, pin lengths of ribbon in place to spell out the word 'shoes', or your own choice of words.

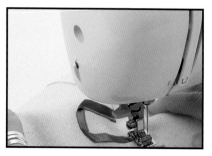

4. Choosing a thread to match the colour of the ribbon, set your sewing machine to do a narrow zigzag stitch that will catch the edge of the ribbon and attach it neatly to the background fabric. Stitch all round each letter.

5. To make up the bag, place front and back pieces right sides together and sew up the two sides and along the bottom, approximately 1.5 cm (1/2 in) from raw edges. Clip corners and turn right sides out. Make a 1.5 cm (1/2 in) double hem at the top. Inside the bag, about 5 cm (2 in) from the top edge, stitch a length of ribbon to form a casing for the cord. Thread the cord through and knot ends. Neaten ends by folding a small piece of ribbon over each one and stitching neatly, to enclose frayed edges.

shoe Bag

A really simple way to form letters is by twisting and folding lengths of ribbon and stitching them in place. What easier way could there be to both decorate and label a functional item such as a shoe bag?

Drawstring bags are an excellent way of organizing and storing clutter, so once you have made a shoe bag or two, why not make a scaled-down version for make-up, hair curlers or tights, or a scaled-up version for towels or laundry, each with its own ribbon-letter label?

Labelled bags not only look attractive, they also make tidying up a lot more fun.

Chalk Board

*P*erfect for children to scribble on or practise their ABCs, a small chalk board also makes a great memo board in the kitchen. You can buy ready-made boards from companies specializing in MDF furnishing blanks, or you can make your own from an offcut of MDF. The instructions below assume that you are starting with a ready-made board, and just explain how to add the alphabet decoration.

The alphabet letters are added by stamping. You can buy sets of alphabet rubber stamps from specialist suppliers and craft shops, or you can make your own by cutting out letters from thin sheets of foam rubber or neoprene, also available from craft shops. The foam rubber letters in the photograph were sold as a set for children to play with in the bath or paddling pool.

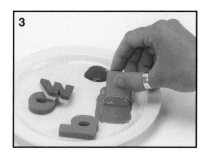

You will need

Plain MDF plaque or memo board
Blackboard paint
Fine-grade sandpaper
Acrylic paints
Foam rubber alphabet stamps
Polyurethane varnish

How to make a chalk board

1. Measure a central rectangle and paint with blackboard paint. Leave to dry.

2. Mask off the edges of the blackboard area, and paint the remainder of the board with two or three layers of acrylic paint, sanding lightly between each layer.

Choose a slightly different colour for each layer, for a distressed finish.

3. Spread some acrylic paint on a plate.

4. Press one of the foam letter shapes into the paint. Apply it to the frame with firm, even pressure, then carefully lift off.

5. Repeat with other letters, using different colours and leaving a little space between them, until the frame is covered.

6. Leave to dry, then protect the frame, but not the area painted with blackboard paint, with a coat or two of varnish.

...ts and rubber stamps turn a piece of scrap wood into a delightful
...k board for childish scribbles.

Home Sweet Home

Alphabets are not just for the nursery but for every other room in the house. Use letters decoratively on furniture and fabrics. Use them in a practical way to identify personal items such as bedlinen, towels and napkins. And use them in a quirky way to convey messages or add a touch of humour to everyday objects.

Bookends

Cardboard

Scissors or craft knife

Sticky tape

Emulsion paint or gesso primer

Acrylic paints

PVA glue

Paintbrushes

Gold paint or gilding cream

Clear polyurethane varnish

Rags

*I*t is always particularly satisfying to create something out of nothing. Papier mâché is one of the most enjoyable and rewarding of the recycling crafts, producing excellent results for very little outlay.

This pair of bookends is made from cardboard boxes and old newspapers. Admittedly, you may have to spend some money on a tube of gold paint or gilding cream, but you could always paint your bookends a bright colour, using paints you already have to hand. In addition to the bookends, a free-standing letter can be placed on the mantelpiece or be hung on the wall.

How to make a papier-mâché bookend

1. Choose a letter with a simple, bold shape. Enlarge it on a photocopier, cut out and stick to a sheet of thick card, or trace around the outline with a pencil.

2. Cut out the shape, using a craft knife. It is advisable to use a steel ruler when cutting straight edges.

3. Cut out several more shapes and tape them together until you achieve the desired thickness. Cut two rectangles of thick card. The upright piece should be at least as tall as the cutout letter and the base should be at least as wide. To make it sturdy, reinforce with extra layers

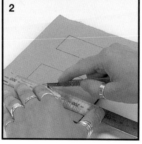 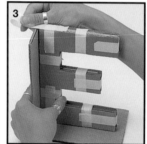  

of cardboard if necessary. Tape the letter shape in place.

4. Dilute the PVA glue, two parts glue to one part water, and paint it all over the cardboard form. Cover with small, torn strips of newspaper, building up at least three or four layers. Leave to dry.

5. Paint with a coat of emulsion or primer. Leave to dry.

6. Paint the whole thing with black acrylic paint. Leave to dry.

7. Brush with a coat of gold paint. Using a clean rag, dab the paint to create a mottled effect. Alternatively, apply a little gilding cream to a rag

and rub into the surface. Allow to dry and buff with a clean cloth.

8. Protect with one or two coats of acrylic varnish, allowing it to dry between coats.

TIPS

Allow the paper and glue to dry thoroughly – for about three to five days, depending on temperature and humidity – before painting. When you paint your model with emulsion paint or gesso primer, cracks may appear in the paint's surface as it dries, but do not worry, as these will be covered up by subsequent layers of paint.

Gold paint is available in several forms. Poster paint is inexpensive and perfectly adequate as long as you protect the surface with a couple of coats of varnish. Acrylic is available in various shades of gold and can be manipulated by brushing or dabbing to create a textured effect. Gilding cream produces a lovely sheen and a little goes a long way.

What could be more fitting for a pair of bookends than three-dimensional alphabet letters?

Cardboard Clock

*T*he positions of the numbers on a clock face are so familiar that, even if you take them away, people can still tell the time. Why not replace them with a cheerful message and create a quirky clock to grace any shelf or mantelpiece?

The raw materials for the clock cost next to nothing. You will just need to acquire a battery-operated movement, which can be purchased from a well-stocked craft shop or from a watch mender. Alternatively, look in your nearest bargain-basement store for a cheap plastic clock, dismantle it and use the movement and hands for your own clockwork creation!

You will need

Round cardboard-box lid

Two cardboard rings

Scrap cardboard

PVA glue

Old newspapers

Paintbrushes

Emulsion paint or gesso primer

Acrylic paints

Pencil

Battery-operated clock movement

How to make a cardboard clock

1. Cut a strip of cardboard the same width as the box lid and long enough to support the box lid and the two cardboard rings laid side by side.

2. Glue the pieces together and leave to dry.

3. Dilute the PVA glue, two parts glue to one part water, and paint it all over the cardboard form. Cover with a layer of small, torn strips of newspaper, paying particular attention to the joins. Paper over the gaps at the base between the three component parts. Leave to dry.

4. Paint with a coat of emulsion or primer. Leave to dry, then paint with a coat of diluted blue acrylic paint.

5. Divide the clock face into twelve equal segments and draw in the letters, using pencil. Fill in the letter shapes with paint, then add other detail. For a distressed look, brush on diluted paint then dab it off with a piece of rag or paper.

6. Protect the painted surface with one or two coats of varnish, allowing it to dry thoroughly between coats.

7. Using a sharp pencil, pierce a hole in the clock face. Remove the hands and push the centre of the clock movement through the hole from the back. Tighten the washer and replace the hands.

TIP

The centre of this clock has been made using the lid from a hat box, with two cardboard spools that once held ribbons on either side. If you haven't got a suitable box lid, try using a cake board. For the side pieces, the cardboard rings from the centres of rolls of sticky tape would be perfect.

TEMPLATES: Clock Face, page 118

*R*ubber stamping is a popular craft, usually used to decorate paper. But by using fabric paints, you can decorate soft furnishings just as simply. Use a shop-bought rubber stamp or make your own – it's easy. Then decorate some bedlinen with a name or a message.

These checked fabrics make a great background, and snuggling down on a pillow printed with 'love' and 'happiness' is sure to conjure up pleasant dreams. If you don't want to tackle a large pillow, print your message on a small sachet and fill it with pot pourri or sweet-smelling dried herbs.

Print your own message on a pillowcase, or make a small, herb-filled pillow for a loved one.

Printed Pillows

You will need

**Checked cotton fabrics,
or ready-made pillowcase**

Alphabet stamps

Fabric paints

Roller or paintbrush

How to print letters

1. Protect your work surface with newspapers. If you are decorating a ready-made pillowcase, put several layers of newspaper inside, so that paint does not soak through to the back.

2. Pour some fabric paint into a saucer. Using a roller or paintbrush, coat the rubber stamp with a thin layer of paint.

3. Before printing your fabric, test the stamp on a spare scrap. When you feel confident enough to tackle the main piece, place the paint-coated stamp gently on to the fabric and apply firm, even pressure. Lift carefully to reveal the printed letter. Repeat with other letters.

To make up a small pillow or sachet

1. Stitch small rectangles of fabric all around the main printed piece to form a border. Cut a piece of fabric the same size to make the back of the cushion.

2. With right sides facing, stitch round three sides, 1 cm ($1/2$ in) from raw edges. Leave one side open for turning. Clip corners and turn right sides out.

3. Fill the pillow with wadding, adding a handful of dried herbs or pot pourri. Tuck in raw edges round opening and slipstitch closed.

Use fabric paints and a simple rubber stamp to print initials on scented sachets.

TIP

Use fabric paints that are water-based and intermixable, so you can create exactly the shade of colour you want. Once fixed, dyes are colourfast and machine washable. To fix the colour, press with a hot iron for the length of time recommended by the manufacturer.

Knitted Patchwork Throw

Novice knitters need not be deterred: only the most rudimentary knitting skills are required to produce simple squares that can be joined together to make a blanket. Extend those skills just slightly and you can decorate the squares with letters of the alphabet.

Just pick up a pair of needles and two shades of yarn, and try. The technique involves knitting rows of stocking stitch – one row plain, one row purl – and following a chart that shows where to put the contrasting coloured stitches. If the idea seems just too daunting, knit plain squares and embroider the letters on afterwards. The throw in the picture is made from thirty-five squares and measures 125 x 95 cm (49 x 37¼ in).

TIP

Any double knitting yarn can be used. A patchwork blanket is a good way of using up small amounts left over from other projects. A single 25 g (1 oz) hank is enough to knit approximately two and a half squares. Use this measurement to calculate how much yarn you are likely to need if you wish to make a smaller or a larger throw.

You will need

17 x 25 g (1 oz) hanks Rowan lightweight DK double knitting wool, in black, white, cream and grey

One pair 4 mm (size 4) knitting needles

Tapestry needle

To make a square

1. Cast on 30 stitches in background colour. Work in stocking stitch (knit first row and every following odd-numbered row; purl second row and every following even-numbered row) for four rows. Carry on working in stocking stitch while at the same time copying your chosen letter, in a second colour of yarn, from the chart on page 119.

2. Make thirty-five squares. Lay out the squares on a flat surface and arrange in seven rows of five squares. Rearrange them until you are pleased with the juxtaposition of colours. Join the squares to make rows, then join the rows together. To do this, oversew edges of squares together, using one strand of yarn in your needle.

3. To make the border, pick up and knit 210 stitches along one long edge of the work. Knit 12 rows in garter stitch (every row knit) and cast off. Repeat on the other long side. On one of the shorter edges, pick up and knit 170 stitches and knit 12 rows in garter stitch, as before. Repeat for the other short edge.

A traditional knitted afghan is given a new twist with lettered squares. Make one from oddments of double knitting yarns to add a cosy touch to a chair or sofa.

TECHNIQUES: Two-colour knitting, page 112.

Outdoor Dining

There are two projects on these pages: personalized napkins and a decorated herb pot, both of which bring a touch of beauty to an outdoor table but would look equally good inside the house.

Initial letters can be embroidered on all kinds of linen but seem particularly appropriate on table napkins, one or more for each family member. Buy ready-made plain napkins, choosing good quality, heavy cotton or linen. Or make your own from squares of thick, coarsely woven 100 per cent cotton, simply hemmed or frayed around the edges.

No step-by-step instructions are given for this; simply trace and transfer the letter of your choice on to the corner of a napkin and fill in the shape with satin stitch, using two strands of 6-stranded embroidery thread in your needle.

A brand-new terracotta pot can be painted to look like an antique. Hand-painted lettering denotes the name of the plant – in Latin – and would make an ideal gift for a keen gardener, not to mention an elegant table centrepiece, filled with fragrant rosemary.

You will need
Large terracotta flower pot
Acrylic paint, white and green
Soft paintbrush
Crackle varnish
Ageing varnish
Oil paint, burnt umber
Rags

How to paint a herb pot

1. Wash and dry the pot. Dilute white acrylic paint with water, about 1 teaspoon of paint to half a cup of water. Brush this liberally all over the outside of the pot. While the paint is still wet, dab it with a dry rag to produce a mottled effect.

2. When the first coat of paint is dry, brush some areas with a little diluted green acrylic, dabbing it off to produce subtle, shaded patches. Leave to dry.

3. Paint the outside of the pot with a coat of crackle varnish. Leave to dry. As it dries, cracks will appear.

4. To show up the cracks in the varnish, and further enhance the aged look, squeeze a small amount of oil paint on to a rag and rub into the surface. Using a clean rag, rub the paint off gently; it will remain in the cracks.

5. Protect with a coat of ageing varnish, or clear polyurethane varnish.

TIPS
Crackle varnish and ageing varnish are available from specialist paint stores and craft shops and are sometimes sold as a two-part kit.
Painted terracotta pots should be protected from damage by frost. In cold weather, either wrap them with fleece or bubble wrap, or bring indoors.

TECHNIQUES: Satin Stitch, page 113
TEMPLATES: Roman Alphabet, page 120

Civilized outdoor eating calls for proper table linen, like these colourful monogrammed napkins. Rosemary, growing in a labelled pot, adds scent to the air.

Bedlinen

When sending bedlinen to a laundry, it is necessary to label each piece with some identifying mark, such as names or initials. There are, however, other reasons for adding letters – there is something very luxurious about crisp white sheets and pillowcases embossed with an elegant monogram.

A monogram can be simple or fancy, a single initial or a string of letters, left plain or embellished with a few swirls or flourishes.

Flowers add a feminine touch. For a man, you may prefer something plainer. Find the lettering you like and trace it on to paper, then play around until you are pleased with the result. Then transfer your artwork on to fabric and stitch. If you use good quality thread and stitch with care, the finished embroidery will be as robust as the bedlinen and can be washed and ironed without worry.

You will need

6-stranded embroidery thread, pale blue, lavender and yellow
Crewel needle
Embroidery hoop
Plain white cotton bedlinen

How to stitch a monogram on bedlinen

1. Choose the position on the sheet or pillowcase, where you want your monogram to be, then transfer your design.

2. Stretch the fabric in an embroidery hoop.

3. Separate the strands of thread and thread your needle with two strands. Fill in the design with satin stitch and stem stitch.

4. Press the embroidery on the reverse of the fabric, using a damp cloth.

TIP
Try out your design on a small scrap of fabric before tackling a bed sheet or pillowcase. This trial piece can be made up into a small, lavender-filled sachet, to scent your linen while it is being stored.

...ell as being pretty, monogrammed ...nen is perfectly practical.

Monogram Pillows

L is for lavender, or love, or maybe it's the initial letter of a loved one.

A monogram can be big or small, simple or intricate, quick to stitch or a labour of love. Here are some pillows made with love, scented with lavender, simply stylish. They are the perfect accessory for your bedroom or sitting room; the perfect gift for someone you care for.

It is easy to enlarge or reduce your chosen letter with the help of a photocopier, to obtain the size you want. Instructions are given for the large linen cushion with the gingham border.

TIP

You may well wish to vary the sizes of your own cushions, from the measurements given here. The large square cushion in the photograph measures 45 cm (18 in), so the cover can be cut from less than half a metre (or half a yard) of fabric. Sachets can be made from oddments of fabric you may have in your work basket.

To calculate the amount of trimming or lace needed to edge a sachet, measure the four sides. The total measurement is the amount of gathered lace needed, plus a little allowance for joining the two ends. If you want to gather flat lace, then allow at least double this length, or three times for a really generous ruffle.

You will need

40 cm (16 in) square of linen fabric

45 cm (18 in) of 90 cm (36 in) wide black-and-white cotton gingham

6-stranded embroidery cotton, white

Embroidery hoop

Crewel needle

White sewing thread

45 cm (18 in) cushion pad

How to make a monogram cushion

1. Transfer your chosen letter, phrase or other design on to the centre of the square of linen.

2. Stretch the fabric in an embroidery hoop and, using two strands of thread in your needle, fill in the letter with satin stitch. When the whole shape has been filled, go round the edge of the letter with a line of backstitch, to make a neat outline.

3. Cut four 7.5 cm (3 in) wide strips of gingham, across the width of the fabric. Use these to form a border around the edge of the linen. Then place the front and back pieces of the cushion together, right sides facing, and stitch around three sides, with a 1.5 cm (½ in) seam. Clip corners and turn the cushion cover right sides out.

4. Insert the cushion pad, tuck in the raw edges and stitch closed.

Stitch an initial, plain or fancy, and make it into a pillow, large or small. Fill it with lavender, then lie back and relax . . .

Mosaic Table

*I*t is remarkable how little pieces of coloured glass tile can transform an otherwise unremarkable piece of furniture. It is also surprising how easy it is to achieve a really excellent result, even if you have never attempted mosaic before.

The only special tool you require is a pair of tile nippers to cut the mosaic tiles. This design uses mostly quartered tiles, so you will have to practise until you are proficient at cutting tiles into four pieces – though it doesn't matter if they are not all perfect squares, as you will need some odd-shaped pieces to fit around awkward curves and corners.

The piece of furniture you choose need not be elegant or expensive but should be sound and strong. It is helpful if, like the table in the photograph, it has a raised edge, to 'frame' the mosaic.

The method described here is for a piece of furniture suitable for occasional outdoor use – but if you leave your table out in all weathers, the grout is liable to crack and the tiles will come unstuck.

Copy the design shown or use your own, sticking to fairly large, bold shapes.

You will need

Small table

Vitreous mosaic tiles, about 1 kg (2.2 lb)

Tile nippers

Pencil

Strong tile adhesive (PVA)

Tile grout

Palette knife

Rags

Acrylic paint

How to make a mosaic table top

1. Prepare the table surface by lightly sanding, to provide a key for the adhesive.

2. Cut tiles into quarters, using tile nippers.

3. Draw your design in pencil on the table top. Working on one area at a time, spread a thick layer of glue over the surface.

4. Stick tile pieces in place, following the pencil lines. Where necessary, cut tiles to shape to fit awkward spaces.

5. Continue until the whole surface of the table is covered with tiles,

then leave overnight, until the glue is completely dry.

6. Spread tile grout all over the tiled area, using a palette knife. Make sure you push the grout into every crevice. Wipe surplus grout from the tiles' surface using a damp rag. Leave overnight, to set.

7. Using a damp rag, wipe over the table top until all traces of grout are removed from the surface of the tiles. Buff with a dry rag, to polish.

8. If necessary, paint the rim and legs of the table with acrylic paint, finishing with a coat of varnish.

...ustomized table sets the mood ...enjoying a quiet cup of coffee. ...at results are easy to achieve, ...nsforming a junk-shop table into ...mart piece of furniture.

TIP

Look out for small splinters of glass when cutting tiles. You should protect your hands with gloves and it may be advisable to wear goggles to protect your eyes.

Decorated Glasses

*H*ere are two simple ideas for decorating glassware. Both methods achieve permanent results, although the glass will not withstand the rigours of the dishwasher and should instead be washed gently by hand in warm, soapy water.

Painted glass makes attractive storage. Even a humble jam jar can be reinvented as a stylish storage container. 'Etched' glass is not really etched at all, but sprayed with a solution that creates a frosted effect. This method looks great on mirrors and windows, too, and is a cheap and effective way of providing privacy in bathrooms, converting plain glass into frosted glass at the touch of a spray-nozzle button.

As well as being useful storage containers, painted glass bottles look lovely displayed with other items of coloured glass.

TIP

Make sure the surface of the glass you are decorating is completely clean, dry and free of dust and grease. Wash first in soapy water, then dry thoroughly with a lint-free cloth.

How to decorate glass jars

You will need

Plain glass jars

Tracing paper

Pebeo Cerne Relief, in black

Pebeo glass paints

Fine paintbrush

1. Copy your chosen letter on to tracing paper. Insert the paper into the jar, positioning the letter exactly where you want it to be.

2. Using the Cerne Relief paint, squeezed straight from the tube, trace the outline of the letter on to the glass. Add an outline, if you wish, following the shape of the jar. Leave to dry for about 2 hours.

3. With the face of the jar which you are decorating in a horizontal position, to prevent drips, fill in the letters with glass paint.

How to create 'etched' glasses

You will need:

Plain glasses

Aerosol glass etch

Paper

Spray Mount temporary adhesive

1. Trace your letter on to paper, or cut letters from a magazine. Spray the reverse side with temporary adhesive and stick in place on the glass.

2. Following the manufacturer's instructions, spray the glass from a distance of about 20 cm (8 in). Leave to dry, then peel off the paper template.

'Etching' glass is quick and easy to do, and it looks very effe[c]

Towel

*C*oloured towels are an essential ingredient in a co-ordinated bathroom scheme. To make yours even more stylish and individual, why not add an embroidered border?

Most towels have a flat strip, contrasting with the thick, looped pile. You could embroider or appliqué straight on to this area. The towels featured here, however, have been embellished with a strip of even-weave fabric embroidered with a cross-stitch alphabet. You can cut a strip of the appropriate length and width from any cross-stitch fabric; alternatively, you can buy special narrow bands of fabric, suitable for cross-stitch embroidery, in a choice of widths and colours, complete with a decorative edging. Ask for Aida band; your local craft shop may also have linen band, which has a finer weave, so the stitches will be smaller.

Instead of a whole alphabet, of course, you could stitch a name, giving each family member his or her own set of towels, or a message, such as 'Don't forget to wash behind your ears!'.

A whole alphabet in neat cross stitch makes a decorative border for a towel.

Add painted lettering to a plain white china soap dish.

How to make a cross-stitch towel border

You will need

Towels, 51 cm (20 in) wide

6 stranded embroidery thread, in matching or contrasting colours

14-count Aida band

Crewel needle

Embroidery hoop (optional)

Sewing thread and needle

1. Cut a length of Aida band 54 cm (21 in) wide. Fold it in half and mark the position of the fold. This centre point should correspond with the centre of your embroidery: the centre point of the alphabet is marked on the chart.

2. Usually, cross stitch is worked with fabric stretch in a hoop. When working on a narrow band of fabric, however, you may prefer not to use a hoop. Starting at the centre, begin working the design, following the chart and using two strands of thread in your needle.

3. Press finished work lightly on the reverse. Pin the band in place on the towel, folding under 1.5 cm (½ in) at each end. Stitch in place.

Stitched on 14-count fabric, the whole alphabet measures 48.5 cm (19 in) in length, so you will need a towel at least this wide. On 12-count fabric, it measures 56 cm (22 in) in length, so you will need a slightly larger towel. Linen band, however, is finer than Aida. On 22-count linen – that is, 22 threads for each 2.5 cm (1 in) of fabric – the alphabet will take up only 30.5 cm (12 in), so can be used to decorate a smaller towel.

Soap Dish

For another individual touch in your bathroom, why not transform a plain white soap dish into a stylish accessory? There are a number of specialist hobby paints available which, when baked in a domestic oven, become permanent. If you're not sure of the steadiness of your hand, practise first. Any mistakes can be wiped away, and you can try again until you are completely happy with your design before baking it.

How to paint a soap dish

You will need

Plain white soap dish

Tracing paper

Soft pencil (4B)

Pebeo Porcelaine 150, Ming Blue

Fine paintbrush

1. Make sure the surface of the dish is clean and grease-free. Draw the lettering in the centre of the dish, using a soft pencil. Draw it freehand, or trace letters from a magazine or other source.

2. Fill in the design using Porcelaine 150 and a fine paintbrush. Add bubbles by dipping the end of a pencil, or the lid of a felt-tip pen, into the paint and carefully pressing it on to the surface of the dish. Leave to dry for at least 24 hours. Remove any remaining pencil marks by rubbing with your fingertip or a soft cloth.

3. Bake the dish in a preheated oven at 160°C/325°F/Gas Mark 5 for 35 minutes, according to the paint manufacturer's instructions.

TEMPLATES: Cross-Stitch Chart, page 112
TECHNIQUES: Cross Stitch, page 113

Découpage Boxes

A few scraps of paper pasted on to a plain box can effect a stunning transformation. The technique is known as découpage, and the secret lies in covering the paper with several coats of varnish for a really smooth finish.

Start with a wooden or sturdy cardboard box and choose letters cut from wrapping paper or paper of a similar weight. If you want to use lettering from a magazine or newspaper, you may find that, once pasted, the print shows through from the other side. Therefore it is a good idea to make a photocopy and use this instead.

You will need

Blank boxes, wood or cardboard

White emulsion or gesso primer

Acrylic paints

Paper cutouts, including lettering and music manuscripts

PVA glue

Small, pointed scissors

Paintbrushes

Crackle varnish

Ageing varnish

Rags

Clear polyurethane varnish

Oil paint, burnt umber

A special two-part varnish cracks as it dries; the cracks are enhanced by rubbing in brown oil paint, which increases the aged appearance.

How to decorate a box with découpage

1. Paint the box with a base colour of white emulsion or gesso primer. Allow to dry.

2. Paint the outside of the box with cream acrylic (mix white paint with a little yellow, adding a touch of red or brown until you achieve a shade you are happy with). Paint the inside of the box black or dark brown, to contrast. Leave to dry for about 2 hours.

3. Meanwhile, cut out a selection of paper scraps to fit the box.

4. Mix PVA glue with a little water, about two parts glue to one part water, and paint this on the back of each paper scrap. Press into position and smooth out any wrinkles or air bubbles. Leave to dry.

5. Brush with a coat of crackle varnish. Leave to dry. As it dries, cracks will appear.

6. To enhance the cracks in the varnish, squeeze a small amount of oil paint on to a rag and rub into the surface.

7. Using a clean rag, rub the paint off gently; some will remain in the cracks.

8. Brush with a coat of ageing varnish and leave to dry. Add two or more coats of clear polyurethane varnish, allowing each coat to dry thoroughly before applying the next.

TIP

There are a number of mail-order companies specializing in blank boxes made from wood or cardboard which are ready to decorate, needing no special preparation. Junk shops and markets are a good source of items ready for rejuvenation, but old layers of paint and varnish will need to be stripped away or sanded off before you begin to paint or decorate.

Words and Pictures

A picture says a thousand words, or so the saying goes, but words make interesting pictures in their own right. You may prefer the impact of a single letter isolated in a frame, a few perfect lines of poetry, or a complete, splendid alphabet. In this chapter you will find some ideas to get you motivated, not only for pictures but for frames, too.

Collage

*M*agazines are an excellent source of visual material. Once you have finished reading your favourite magazine, and before you consign it to the recycling bin, take a few minutes to tear out any pages containing interesting type, or large areas of flat colour.

This picture, made entirely from coloured pieces cut from magazines, has lots of impact, is very original, and yet it cost next to nothing to make. The only cost was the picture mount and frame which, being a ready-made one from a department store, was relatively inexpensive.

If the bright, bold colours in this example are not to your taste, choose your own palette. Once you have cut out a good selection of pieces from your magazine, have fun arranging and rearranging them until you come up with a pleasing pattern. Then just stick them down and you have an original work of art!

You will need

Letters and scraps cut from magazines

Frame with cardboard mount

Piece of cardboard or thick paper

Pencil

Ruler

Glue stick

How to make a collage

1. Cut a piece of cardboard or thick paper to fit your frame. Place the mount on top and mark the aperture in the centre. Divide this area into squares of approximately 4 cm (1½ in).

2. Cut out plain coloured squares from magazine scraps, each the same size as the squares on your grid.

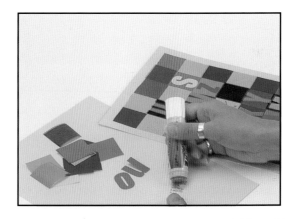

3. Stick the squares in place using the glue stick. Then stick a letter in each square.

ers cut from magazines and arranged in a grid
e a surprisingly effective, modern picture.

Word Frames

To add an extra dimension when framing a photograph, why not add some words? This could be in the form of a caption or, more subtly, the words could form a frame around the picture, not necessarily meaning to be read but adding a touch of sentimentality, nostalgia or perhaps even humour or wit.

The photograph of pink tulips in a silver frame has been superimposed on a sheet of pink paper, printed with 'pink' words: rose, raspberry, lilac, peach, sugar and so on. The idea could be varied for other colours: shades of blue, green and so on. The words were generated on a computer and printed using an inkjet colour printer. If you do not have access to such equipment, similar effects could be achieved by hand-writing words on coloured paper, using a felt-tip pen, by stencilling or stamping letters, or by transforming black type into coloured type with the aid of a colour photocopier.

The photograph in the small gilt frame at the front has been put behind a cardboard mount, the mount having been covered with a photocopy of a letter in attractive script handwriting. Old postcards from junk shops are a good source of lovely handwriting. Try blowing them up on a photocopier. If you feel the words themselves detract attention from the photograph in the centre, get a reverse photocopy made, so that you have the visual appeal of the script without the distraction of the meaning.

In the larger gilt frame, an undamaged page has been torn from an old book which would otherwise have been thrown away. A coloured scrap, a reproduction of a Victorian label, is stuck on top of this. The combination of the words on the label – 'To the loved ones at home' – and the old text, creates a very sentimental piece.

Words add an extra dimension framed pictures, transforming simple snapshot into somethin very special.

Illustrated Alphabet

After we first learn the alphabet, the next step is associating letters with words. A is for apple, artichoke and armadillo – but in this picture, A is for anchor, B is for bicycle, C for car and so on.

Trace the alphabet from page 124, or customize it with your own choice of pictures. This alphabet has been embroidered, but you could just as easily trace it on to a piece of card and colour in the letter shapes with paints or felt-tip pens. You could even trace a single square, with the initial letter of your choice, to make a smaller picture or a greetings card.

You will need

35 x 30 cm (13³/₄ x 11³/₄ in) plain white cotton fabric

Pencil or erasable pen

6-stranded embroidery thread in black, yellow, green, turquoise blue, cobalt blue, orange, red and lavender

Crewel needle

Embroidery hoop

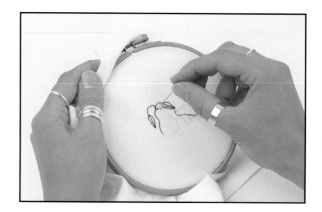

How to stitch an alphabet picture

1. Enlarge the design to the required size. Lay the fabric on top and trace, using a pencil or erasable pen.

2. Mount the fabric in an embroidery hoop. Stitch the pictures in stem stitch and backstitch, using one strand of black thread.

3. With two strands of thread in the needle, fill in the letters in satin stitch, using the finished picture in the photograph as a guide to colour.

4. Press the completed work on the reverse.

TIP

Have the embroidery professionally framed, or do it yourself with a ready-made frame. Cut a piece of card to fit the frame and stretch the embroidery over the card, securing it at the back by stitching or using either fabric glue or sticky tape, before placing it in the frame.

A is for anchor, B is for bicycle and so on in this embroidered picture, perfect for the nursery but sophisticated enough for other rooms in the house.

TEMPLATES: Illustrated Alphabet, page 124
TECHNIQUES: Satin Stitch, Stem Stitch, page 113

Mirror Frame

*H*ere is an idea for decorating any plain wooden frame. The one featured in the photograph was sold as a plain MDF frame, complete with mirror. You could buy a similar blank frame from a specialist supplier, or hunt for a mirror with an interestingly shaped frame in a junk shop or flea market.

If the frame is already painted or varnished, you will have to 'key' the surface by sanding it. If, however, the frame is made from untreated, unpainted wood or MDF, it is ready to be painted and decorated.

You will need

Mirror with plain wooden frame

Gesso primer or white emulsion paint

Acrylic paints, in white and pink

Fine-grade sandpaper

Medium paintbrush

Letters cut from magazines

PVA glue

Polyurethane varnish

How to decorate a mirror frame

1. Protect the mirror with a piece of paper held in place with strips of masking tape. Paint the frame with a coat of gesso primer or emulsion paint. Leave to dry.

2. Paint the frame with white acrylic and the edge in a contrasting colour, in this case pink.

3. Cut out letters and words from magazines.

4. Dilute PVA by mixing two parts of PVA with one part of water. Brush the mixture on to the back of each letter and apply to the frame, then brush a little more of the mixture over the top of the letter. Leave to dry.

5. Protect the frame with a coat or two of varnish, allowing it to dry thoroughly between coats.

TIP

For a distressed finish, after painting the frame with primer, paint with a coat of pink acrylic, then a coat of white. Sand lightly to reveal some of the colour beneath.

esn't have to mean anything: random
rs just provide decorative detail on a
ted wooden mirror frame.

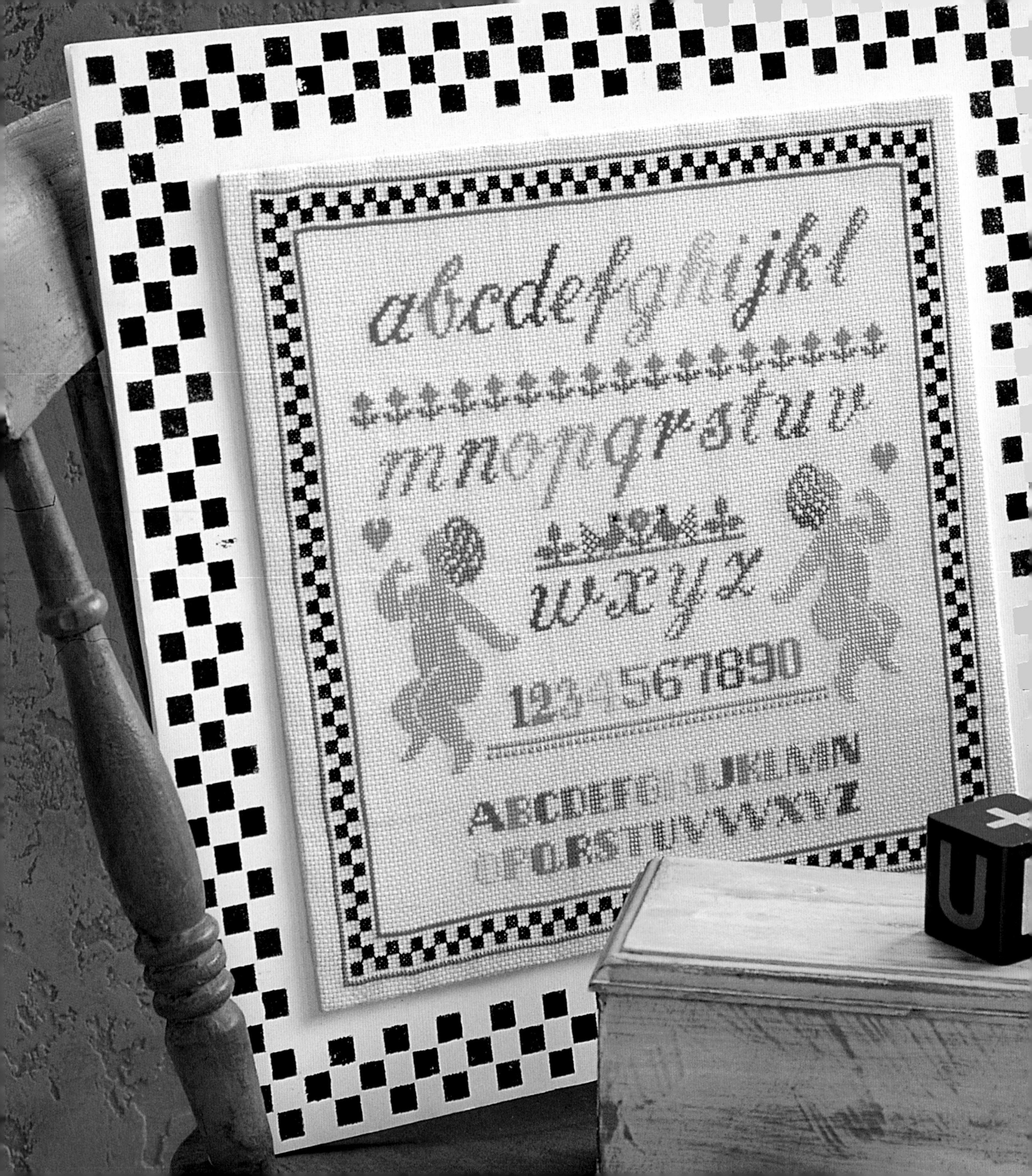
abcdefghijkl
mnopqrstuv
wxyz
1234567890

Cross-Stitch Samplers

*F*or centuries samplers have been stitched, mainly by children, as exercises in embroidery. Alphabets are a recurring theme of cross-stitch samplers, alongside other decorative devices. In recent years, cross stitch has enjoyed a major revival in popularity.

If you have not yet attempted this simple embroidery technique, what better way to start than with an alphabet, worked in neat rows? The finished result, simply framed, will add a touch of nostalgia to your home.

The alphabet sampler has infinite variations. You can keep it plain or add borders and embellishments. You can stick to one colour, or two, or be bold and brave and use a whole rainbow.

You will find several cross-stitch charts at the back of the book, complete with sizes and amounts of fabrics and threads needed to make each one. The instructions given below apply to all the charts.

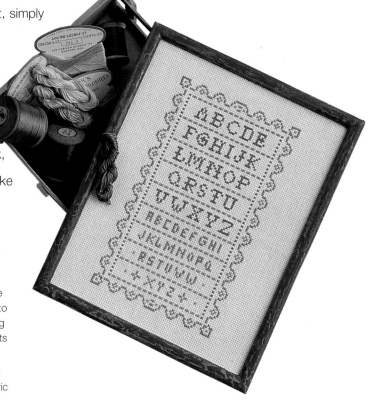

How to stitch a cross-stitch sampler
You will need
Cross-stitch fabric
6-stranded embroidery thread
Tapestry needle no. 24
Embroidery hoop

1. Mark the centre of your fabric by folding it in half both vertically and horizontally and stitching along the folds, in running stitch, using a single strand of thread. These lines can be removed once you have begun stitching your design.

2. Stretch the fabric in an embroidery hoop.

3. With two strands of thread in your needle, begin to stitch from the centre of the design, following the chart. The centre is indicated by arrows which correspond to your vertical and horizontal lines of running stitch. Each square on the chart represents a single cross stitch.

4. Once you have finished, iron your work lightly on the reverse. If you place the fabric on a folded towel, it helps to prevent the stitches being flattened.

5. Before framing the work, stretch it over a piece of acid-free cardboard, securing it at the back by stitching or with fabric glue or sticky tape.

TIP
Most professional picture framers will be able to mount and frame embroidered pieces. If you want to do it yourself, simply stretch the finished work, as described in step 5, above, over a piece of cardboard that will fit your chosen frame. The sampler with the chequered border on the facing page was mounted in this way, then glued to the centre of a larger piece of thick mounting board. The chequered pattern was created using a stencil and black acrylic paint.

Alphabets to Wear

*A*ll kinds of labels, logos and slogans adorn our clothes nowadays but you can dare to be different by adding your own wording. Use lettering as pure decoration, as a subtle way of conveying a message or as a more obvious form of expression.

Appliqué Skirt

*E*very little girl loves to have something special to wear. And what could be more special than a swirly skirt with letters that spell out her name? Letters cut from cotton fabrics, stitched in place, will stand up to plenty of wear and tear and frequent laundering, making this garment practical as well as pretty.

You will need

Cotton fabrics

Sewing thread in colours to match fabrics

60 cm (23 3/4 in) flat elastic, 25 mm (1 in) wide

How to make an appliqué skirt

1. To make the skirt, cut a rectangle of fabric measuring 116 cm (45 3/4 in) by 48 cm (19 in). Join the two short ends to form a cylinder.

2. Turn under 4 cm (1 1/2 in) on the top edge and press. Turn under the same amount again, to form a double hem. Sew in place with a line of stitching close to the lower fold, leaving a small gap to insert elastic. Stitch a second line of stitching close to the top edge. The two lines of stitching form a casing for the elastic.

3. Cut a length of elastic measuring 51 cm (20 in) or long enough to go around the child's waist with a small overlap. Insert the elastic, overlap ends and stitch.

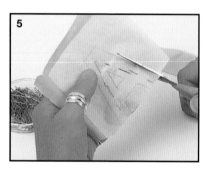

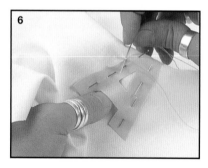

4. Fold, press and stitch a double hem at the bottom of the skirt.

5. Cut out simple letter shapes from scraps of cotton fabric, using a variety of colours. Pin letters in place along lower edge of skirt. Baste in place and remove pins.

6. To stitch letters to backing fabric, tuck under about 1–2 mm (1/16 – 1/8 in) of the raw edge of the fabric, using the point of your needle, and slipstitch in place, using matching thread and making your stitches as small and neat as possible. Remove basting stitches and press.

TIP

The measurements given are for a skirt to fit a child aged five or six. As the skirt is so simple to make, it is easy to make it correspondingly smaller or larger. Just measure the child's waist and cut a rectangle of fabric twice this measurement and as wide as the length you want the skirt to be, allowing for a hem. You could also, of course, apply letters to a shop-bought skirt.

TEMPLATES: Block Alphabet, page 121

Waistcoat

*E*ven the most conservative dresser can feel comfortable in a waistcoat made from a fancy fabric. In fact, in all walks of life, waistcoats seem to be the chosen garment of self-expression.

This waistcoat features word labels made by transferring photocopied images from magazines directly on to the fabric. If the style is too avant-garde for you, just decorate a T-shirt or a shoe bag instead – the technique is the same.

The method reverses the original image, so it is important to obtain a reversed photocopy of any lettering you wish to transfer.

How to make a decorated waistcoat

1. Using the paper pattern, cut out the pieces of the waistcoat from white fabric.

2. Protect your work surface with newspapers. Trim the photocopied images to the shape and size you want, then cover it with a coat of the image transfer solution, brushing it on thickly and evenly.

3. Place the waistcoat fronts face up on a piece of aluminium foil or plastic, then place the coated picture face down on the fabric.

Cover with a piece of kitchen paper and press down, using a roller.

4. Remove the kitchen paper and leave to dry for at least 4 hours, or overnight.

5. Remove the paper from the transfer by rubbing with a damp sponge, then leave to dry. Rub a little more of the solution on to the transferred image, to form a protective film.

6. Make up the waistcoat according to the pattern instructions. When pressing, avoid touching the image areas with the hot iron.

You will need

Plain white cotton fabric

Waistcoat pattern

Aluminium foil or plastic bags

Kitchen paper

Old newspapers

Dylon Image Maker transfer solution

Paintbrush

Roller

TIPS
Follow the manufacturer's instructions carefully when using the transfer solution. Even novice dressmakers can tackle a simple waistcoat. There is no room here to provide a pattern, but easy-to-follow paper patterns are widely available.

a subtle statement
old one with a
-made waistcoat.
an create a really
dual garment by this
e transfer method.

T-shirts

*S*hop-bought or home-made rubber stamps can be used to print an all-over pattern on a plain T-shirt, with fabric paints. You can print a whole alphabet or repeat a single letter, use one colour or several. Instead of a random pattern, you could, of course, print a message, greeting or slogan. On a large T-shirt, there may even be room for a whole poem!

You will need

Plain cotton T-shirts

Old newspapers and cardboard

Alphabet stamps

Fabric paints

Roller or paintbrush

How to print a T-shirt

1. Protect your work surface with newspapers. Place a sheet of cardboard inside the T-shirt, to keep the fabric taut and prevent paint from soaking through to the back.

2. Pour some fabric paint into a saucer. Using a roller or paintbrush, coat the rubber stamp with a thin layer of paint.

3. Before printing, test the stamp on a spare scrap of fabric or paper. When you feel confident enough to tackle your garment, place the paint-coated stamp gently on to the fabric and apply firm, even pressure. Lift carefully to reveal the printed letter. Repeat.

TIPS

Use water-based fabric paints and mix them together, if necessary, to create exactly the shade of colour you want.

Before printing, wash, dry and press the T-shirt, to remove any dressing and to soften the fabric so that the dyes penetrate the fibres.

Print a plain T-shirt with a single letter, repeated in bright colours, or a random selection in monochrome for a stylish fashion statement.

silk scarf

Handwriting, or script, forms an abstract pattern in the drapes and folds of a scarf, so you could be wearing a poem or a love letter around your neck and only you would know what was written there: everyone else would just see patterns and colours. Unless, of course, you decide to open it out flat and expose your secret.

The method used here employs a substance called gutta. This soaks into the fabric so that when colour is applied it cannot seep into these areas.

You will need
Plain silk scarf
Vanishing marker pen
Wooden frame
Gutta
Soft paintbrush
Pebeo silk paints

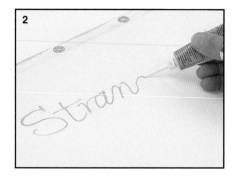

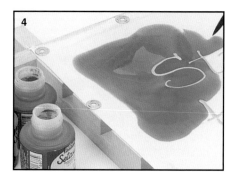

How to decorate a silk scarf

1. If you need some guidelines on the fabric before applying the gutta, draw your lettering freehand, or trace it on to the scarf, using a vanishing marker pen.

2. Stretch the scarf on a wooden frame. Trace over the lines you have drawn, using gutta.

Make sure the gutta sinks into the fabric. Leave to dry for about 1 hour.

3. Using a soft paintbrush, sweep colour over the design. You do not have to paint right up to the gutta lines, as the dye will bleed into the fabric, stopping when it meets the gutta.

4. Use several shades of one colour, allowing them to bleed into one another; this will create an interesting, subtly patterned background to the script.

5. Leave to dry, then press with a hot iron to fix the dyes. Wash and press before wearing.

TIPS

Use gutta straight from the tube or pour it into a small plastic bottle and attach a fine nozzle for more delicate lines. Gutta can be colourless but is also available in a range of colours.

It is advisable to wash, dry and press your scarf before you apply the gutta. This will remove any dressing from the fabric, allowing the gutta to sink into the fibres. Of course, you do not have to use a ready-made scarf. A length of white or ivory silk would be ideal – crêpe de chine, chiffon or a similar soft, draping fabric – and you just have to hem the edges afterwards.

For a subtle message that you can carry with you, paint a poem or song lyrics on to a silk scarf.

Edible Alphabets

P reparing something special to eat is a
recognized way to show that you care.
Special occasions are a wonderful chance to
be particularly creative in the kitchen and an
ideal time to send a message than can not
only be read but eaten, too.

Alphabet Soup

Children seem to like pasta, most grown-ups enjoy a comforting bowl of soup, and the novelty of alphabet letters makes this dish pretty irresistible. The soup, made from healthy ingredients, serves at least four people, is inexpensive as well as quick and easy to prepare, and suitable for vegetarians. Of course, some people will be tempted to cheat, bypassing the recipe and stirring cooked alphabet pasta into shop-bought soup. It doesn't really matter – it will be just as much fun!

You will need

30 ml (2 tbsp) olive oil

1 large onion

1 garlic clove

1 celery stalk

2 large carrots

2 x 400g (14 oz) cans tomatoes

30 ml (2 tbsp) tomato purée

500ml (1 pint) vegetable stock

Salt and pepper

75g (3 oz) alphabet pasta

How to make alphabet soup

1. Chop the onion, garlic and celery. Heat the oil in a large saucepan and cook the onion, garlic and celery over a medium heat, stirring frequently, until soft and transparent but not browned.

2. Stir in the tomato purée. Chop the carrots and add them, with the tomatoes and their juice, the stock and seasoning.

Bring to the boil, then lower the heat, cover and simmer for 20 minutes.

3. In a blender or food processor, blend the soup until smooth, then return it to the pan. Heat to boiling point, then add the pasta and cook over a medium heat for a further 10 minutes, until the pasta is cooked.

A tasty bowl of tomato and carrot soup is made more hearty and substantial – and much more fun – by the addition of pasta letters!

Carved Melon

*F*or any kind of celebration, a carved watermelon makes not only an eyecatching centrepiece but also the perfect container for a juicy fruit salad. Using a simple lino-cutting or wood-engraving tool, carve your own message, appropriate to the occasion. You'll need a steady hand and, if you're not sure of your carving skills, have a spare melon handy in case of mistakes.

You will need

Watermelon

White or light-coloured chinagraph pencil

Lino-cutting or wood-engraving tool

How to carve a melon

1. Write your chosen lettering design freehand on the melon skin, or trace it on to paper and transfer.

2. Carefully gouge out the skin, following the lines you have drawn. Take your time. Start by scooping out a thin, shallow line, then go over it until you have achieved the required depth and thickness.

3. Wipe off any remaining pencil lines using a damp cloth. Store the melon in the refrigerator.

TIP

The carving can be done a day in advance. Just before serving, cut off the top of the melon and scoop out the flesh. Discard the seeds, chop the flesh and add other fresh fruits such as halved apricots, orange segments, seeded grapes, chopped nectarines and peaches, and sliced kiwi fruits.

...ding on a bed of vine ...es, what a refreshing way ...onvey a heartfelt greeting!

Shaped Biscuits

For a children's party, home-baked sweet biscuits will brighten up the tea table, and, if you mark each star with a child's initial, it will help to avoid squabbles. For smaller biscuit nibbles, use canapé cutters to create whole alphabets, then use them to spell out names and birthday messages. The icing sets hard, so biscuits could be wrapped and slipped into party bags at going-home time.

The quantity of biscuit dough given will make about twelve stars and 150 tiny letters, depending on the sizes of cutters used.

You will need

500 g (1 lb) plain flour, plus extra for dusting

Pinch of salt

300 g (10 oz) butter, diced, plus extra for greasing

250 g (8 oz) caster sugar

2 eggs, lightly beaten

250 g (8 oz) icing sugar, sifted

15 ml (1 tbsp) lemon juice

Food colouring

How to make shaped biscuits

1. Sift the flour and salt into a large mixing bowl. Add the butter and rub between your fingers until the mixture resembles fine breadcrumbs.

2. Stir in the sugar. Make a well in the centre of the mixture and add the eggs. Mix to form a soft dough.

3. Turn the dough on to a lightly floured surface and knead gently until smooth. Wrap in cling film and refrigerate for about 20 minutes or until needed.

4. Heat the oven to 180°C/350°F/Gas Mark 4. Roll out the dough on a lightly floured surface to a thickness of 5 mm (1/4 in). Cut out shapes, rerolling the dough as necessary. Place shapes on greased baking sheets and bake for 5–6 minutes, until golden. Leave for 2 minutes, then transfer to a wire rack and leave to cool completely before decorating.

5. In a medium bowl, add the lemon juice to the icing sugar and stir until well mixed. Add a few drops of water, if necessary, to make a thick spreading consistency. Spread a little icing over each biscuit. Add a drop or two of food colouring to the icing remaining in the bowl, spoon into a piping bag with a small, plain nozzle and pipe initials and other decorations on to each star biscuit. Leave to set.

TIPS

Cake decorating shops and many supermarkets sell coloured icing in small plastic tubes. Easy to use, it can be squeezed straight from the tube.

If you haven't got a star-shaped biscuit cutter, make a cardboard template, place it on the dough and cut around it using the tip of a sharp knife.

TEMPLATE: Star, page 125

An alphabet theme perfect for a child's birthday tea – every guest will know which is his or her biscuit

Small Cakes

Set the table for a traditional tea with a twist. Iced fairy cakes are popular with young and old, and in this case they are made even more special by piping everyone's initials on top.

Add a few dainty sandwiches, get out the best china and your antique lace tablecloth, put the kettle on, and there you have it: a tea that grandmother would have been proud of.

You will need

50 g (2 oz) self-raising flour

50 g (2 oz) cornflour

5 ml (1 level tsp) baking powder

50 g (2 oz) butter, at room temperature

50 g (2 oz) caster sugar

1 egg, beaten

15 ml (1 tbsp) milk

12 paper cake cases

175 g (6 oz) icing sugar

15–30 ml (1–2 tbsp) lemon juice

Food colouring, pink

How to make small cakes

1. Heat the oven to 190°C/375°F/Gas Mark 5. Sieve the flour, cornflour and baking powder into a bowl.

2. In a separate large bowl, cream together the butter and sugar, using a wooden spoon, until light and fluffy.

3. Add some of the egg to the creamed mixture and beat in well. Beat in a little of the flour. Continue in this way, alternately beating in egg and flour, to give a smooth mixture. Finally, beat in the milk.

4. Place the paper cases on a baking tray and spoon the mixture into them.

Bake for 7–10 minutes, until well risen, golden and springy to the touch. Remove from the oven and transfer to a wire rack to cool.

5. When the cakes are completely cold, decorate them. Sift the icing sugar into a bowl and mix in enough lemon juice to make a thick, spreading consistency. Transfer about one third of the mixture to a piping bag fitted with a star nozzle. Put aside. Colour the remaining icing pink by adding a drop of food colouring. Use a palette knife to spread the icing over the tops of the cakes, then use the piping bag to pipe an initial on top of each one.

ake any teatime special occasion 'th daintily iced 'ry cakes.

TIP

If you don't like the idea of using artificial food colouring, turn the icing pink by adding raspberry juice. Just press a few ripe berries through a nylon sieve.

Tea Cosy

A tea cosy keeps the teapot warm. This one features a nursery rhyme all about making tea, and although the embroidery looks very intricate, it is actually very easy to do.

You will need

Anchor 6-stranded embroidery cotton, one skein each of blue 433, pink 57, green 239, green 255, purple 111, pale blue 130, lavender 109, yellow 289, black 403, white 2, greys 274, 847, 848, 900 and 8581

35 x 30 cm (13³/₄ x 11³/₄ in) plain white cotton fabric

Crewel embroidery needle

Embroidery hoop

Cotton fabric for backing and lining

35 x 60 cm (13³/₄ x 23³/₄ in) medium-weight wadding

White thread for quilting

1.7 m (67 in) of 25 mm (1 in) bias binding

50 cm (19³/₄ in) ribbon

1 small button

How to make an embroidered tea cosy

1. Copy the design on to the fabric, either by tracing or transferring.

2. Mount the fabric in an embroidery hoop. With two strands of thread in the needle, fill in the larger lettering in satin stitch, using shades of blue and purple.

3. For the flower garland, stitch the stems in stem stitch, using light green thread, and the leaves and flowers in satin stitch.

4. For the teapot, cup and kettle, start with small details such as the flower and leaf pattern, then fill in the large areas in long and short stitch. For shaded areas, combine two strands of different colours in your needle.

5. Finally, with a single strand of black, work the small lettering in backstitch.

6. When the embroidery is complete, press on the reverse, then trim the fabric to shape by cutting off the two top corners in a curve. Cut three more pieces in the same shape from contrasting fabric. Place one of these pieces face down. Place a piece of wadding, cut to shape, on top, then the embroidered piece face up on top of this.

7. Pin and baste all three pieces together, then quilt with lines of running stitch following the contours of the embroidered shapes.

8. Sandwich the second piece of wadding between the remaining two pieces of fabric and stitch these together with several lines of quilting.

9. Bind the lower (straight) edges of both quilted pieces with bias binding. Join the two halves by stitching close to raw edges, up the sides and along the top. Cover the seam with remaining bias binding.

10. As a finishing touch, tie the ribbon in a bow and stitch to the top, adding a small button.

Keep the tea warm with a prettily embroidered cover, perfect for preserving the traditions of teatime!

Celebration Cake

*E*very once in a while, a birthday, anniversary, christening or wedding calls for a special party, with a celebration cake as the centrepiece. Whether you choose a fruit cake, a sponge or a delicious chocolate confection is up to you. But here is a decorating idea that is appropriate for any occasion: a message or names piped in coloured icing around the cake.

The letters could spell out good wishes, or the name of a baby, or the names of the happy couple celebrating their wedding or anniversary. Whatever you choose to say, this is an easy but very effective way to do it.

Use royal icing – icing sugar mixed with egg white – for the best results, adding a few drops of food colouring, if you wish, to make the lettering stand out from the white cake. Then add some fresh flowers on top of the cake, to echo the colours of the icing.

As a lasting memento of the occasion, the cake pictured stands on a cloth embroidered with a monogram. A few sample monograms are provided at the back of the book, or you can make up your own. Follow the instructions given for the monogrammed table napkins on page 44. In other words, simply transfer your design on to the corner of your cloth, and fill in with satin stitch, using two strands of 6-stranded embroidery thread in your needle.

Piped icing-sugar letters on a celebration cake are neat and plain, in contrast to the fancy embroidered monogram on the tablecloth.

Gifts and Keepsakes

There are times when we want to send
particular messages – on birthdays,
anniversaries and other special days.
Taking the trouble to make a special gift
or greeting will make these times even
more memorable.

Valentine Heart

A longside a card this Valentine's Day, why not make a plump little fabric love token to send to the object of your desire? Pieced together from the tiniest scraps of fabric and lovingly embroidered with a single initial, it is sure to touch the heart of the one you admire.

Don't worry if your sewing is less than perfect, it will all add to the charm. But if you don't want to embroider the heart, you could stamp an initial using the technique described on page 40.

How to make an embroidered heart

You will need

Scraps of cotton fabrics

6-stranded embroidery thread

Crewel needle

Transfer pen

Wadding

1. Trace the heart template from page 116. If you wish, reduce or enlarge it with the help of a photocopier. Cut out the paper heart to make a pattern.

2. Stitch several squares of fabric together, to form a piece of patchwork slightly larger than the heart pattern. Make sure there is a central patch of plain fabric on which to stitch the monogram.

3. Trace your chosen letter on to thin paper, then draw over the letter on the back of the paper using a transfer pen. Place the design on the fabric and press with a hot iron, to transfer the letter to the fabric.

4. Stretch the fabric in an embroidery hoop. With two strands of embroidery thread in your needle, fill in the letters, using satin stitch for wider areas and stem stitch for thin lines.

5. When the embroidery is complete, press lightly on the reverse. Place on top of another piece of patchwork, or a piece of plain fabric. Pin the paper pattern to both thicknesses, and cut out.

6. Place the two fabric hearts with right sides facing and stitch all round, 1 cm (1/2 in) from raw edges, leaving a small gap in one of the straight sides, for turning. Clip curves and trim off points at the bottom. Turn right sides out.

7. Fill the pillow with wadding, adding a handful of dried herbs or pot pourri, if you wish. Tuck in raw edges around opening and slipstitch closed.

These Valentine cards take very little time to make – hand if you have quite a number to send! Jus stick candy love hearts on to coloure paper, photocopy and cut out.

TEMPLATE: Heart, page 116
TECHNIQUES: Satin Stitch, page 113

Stationery

A small rubber stamp or a set of stencils is all you need to turn a pile of plain paper into personalized stationery.

There are no rules to follow here. The set in the photograph comprises a stack of buff-coloured paper stored in a small wooden box. The box, which once contained toiletries, was given a few coats of acrylic paint and sanded to achieve an aged finish. Follow the instructions given for the mirror frame on page 67. The box and the sheets of paper were then stamped with an old printer's lettering block picked up from an antiques market, and using an ordinary black ink-stamp pad from a stationery shop.

The notebooks, just plain items from a office supply shop, were personalized with a set of stencils and black acrylic paint. You can buy alphabet stencils and rubber stamps from craft shops in a variety of sizes and designs.

The découpage boxes featured on pages 56–57 would complement the items on these pages very well, and a whole, personalized set would make a marvellous gift for a special friend.

Use a small stamp or stencil to turn plain paper into personalized stationery.

Wedding

A wedding is the perfect excuse for extravagance. It is also a chance to use your creativity. A monogram made up from the bride and groom's initials makes a very effective – and appropriate – wedding motif. Use it firstly to make up invitation cards and then to decorate all kinds of other things.

A small pillow, embroidered and lace-trimmed, holds the wedding rings at the ceremony. Paper cones contain confetti or rice. At the reception, china plates are trimmed with embossed lettering and tables decorated with 'his and hers' gold hearts.

You could think of other applications for decorative lettering, too, such as an embroidered garter for the bride, a souvenir album for the wedding photos (see the Christmas Memories album on page 111) or decorated glasses (see page 52–53).

How to make confetti cones

1. Draw your design as black outline letters on white paper. Photocopy the design on to sheets of coloured paper. Make sure the design is positioned in the top left-hand corner of each sheet.

2. Using gold paint and a fine brush, fill in the lettering, leaving the black outlines showing.

3. Cut off a 87 mm (3¹/₂ in) strip from the bottom of each piece of paper, to leave a square.

4. Roll each square to form a cone with the design showing at the top. Tape or glue in place. Fill with confetti.

You will need

A4 photocopying paper in pastel colours

Gold acrylic paint or ink

Fine paintbrush

Glue stick or double-sided sticky tape

Confetti

How to make wedding invitations

1. As with the confetti cones, start with a black outline design on white paper. Photocopy the design on to sheets of semi-transparent paper. You should be able to fit several motifs on to one sheet.

2. Using gold paint and a fine brush, fill in, leaving the black outlines showing.

3. Stick wrapping paper on to one side of the card. Cut the card into rectangles measuring 20 x 14 cm (8 x 5¹/₂ in) Stick a lettering motif on to each card.

4. Score each card in half, lengthwise, using a metal ruler and the point of your scissors, then fold.

You will need

Medium-weight white card

Gold acrylic paint or ink

Fine paintbrush

Wrapping paper with calligraphy design

Semi-transparent paper (tracing paper or Japanese paper)

Glue stick or spray

A design made up
of the bride's and
groom's initials can
be used to decorate
any number of
items. Duplicate it
to make invitations,
or embroider it on a
ring pillow.

How to make a ring pillow

You will need

14 x 14 cm (5¹/₂ x 5¹/₂ in) square of cotton or linen

Gold embroidery thread

6-stranded embroidery cotton, pink

Crewel needle

Embroidery hoop

1.2 m (48 in) of 25 mm (1 in) white lace

1.2 m (48 in) of 6 cm (2¹/₂ in) ivory lace

52 x 26 cm (20 x 10 in) ivory fabric

Ivory cotton sewing thread

60 cm (24 in) narrow ivory double satin ribbon

24 cm (9¹/₂ in) square cushion pad

1. Transfer the design on to the square of cotton or linen. Stretch the fabric in an embroidery hoop, then fill in the design with gold thread, in satin stitch.

2. With two strands of pink thread in your needle, stitch a square border in cross stitch, to surround the design.

3. Cut the ivory fabric into two equal-sized squares, to form the front and back of the cushion cover. Place the embroidered square centrally on one piece, and stitch in place close to the edges.

4. Cut the ivory lace into four equal lengths. Taking two of the pieces, place right sides together. Pin. Stitch at a 45-degree angle, to make a mitred corner. Repeat with the other pieces.

5. Stitch this lace 'frame' to the cushion front. Make a second 'frame' of white lace and stitch on top, to hide any raw edges of fabric. Tie the ribbon on to one corner.

6. With right sides together, stitch front to back with a 1 cm (¹/₂ in) seam, leaving a gap for turning. Clip corners, turn right sides out, insert cushion pad and close opening.

How to decorate plates

You will need

China plates with plain coloured rim

Pebeo Porcelaine outliner, gold

Soft pencil

1. Draw out your design freehand, in pencil, on the rim of the plate. Alternatively, draw around the plate on to a piece of paper, to make a template. Draw out your design, then trace over the back with soft pencil, then transfer the design to the plate.

2. Go over the pencil lines with outliner paint, wiping away any mistakes while the paint is still wet. Leave to dry, then wipe away pencil lines with a dry cloth.

TIPS

Sizes given are approximate. For example, you may want to make invitation cards narrower or wider, depending on your own motif or the size of envelope available.

The ring pillow, too, could be made smaller, if you prefer. You could use scraps of lace left over from making the bridal gown. You could also add extra layers of lace or ribbons to make the pillow more elaborate.

If you decorate plates with Pebeo Porcelaine, it will dry hard and the plates can be used once, then the designs washed off. Alternatively, the decorated plates can be baked in a domestic oven to make the design permanent.

Buy heart decorations or make your own from papier maché, using the method described for the bookends on page 36. Then decorate with outliner paint, as for the plates.

TECHNIQUES: Satin Stitch, page 113

Use dimensional paint to create luxurious raised designs on plates and decorations for the wedding feast.

Thank You

A greetings card is sometimes not quite good enough when you want to send a special message. Words of thanks, simply stitched on to a little pillow, will outlast most other forms of greeting.

Here is an embroidered pillow, with the words 'thank you' in a pretty script embellished with swirls and swashes. And there's a little needlepoint cushion where alphabet letters are coupled with a heart motif. Choose your own initial or combination of letters and increase the size of the pillow by increasing the number of squares worked.

TIPS

In the example photographed, the colours of the embroidery match the flowers on the braid. A skein of embroidery thread, dyed in shades of red and pink was used. If you cannot find shaded thread, use several different shades for different parts of the lettering, to achieve a similar effect.

If you want to say a really big 'thank you', make your message last by embroidering it and making it into a little scented pillow.

How to make an embroidered pillow

You will need

White cotton fabric

90 cm (1 yd) of 2.5 cm (1 in) wide cotton braid

6-stranded embroidery thread, in colours to match braid

Embroidery hoop

Crewel needle

Pencil, or transfer pen

White sewing thread

Wadding

Lavender or pot pourri

90 cm (1 yd) of cotton picot lace

1. Cut two squares of fabric, each measuring 15 cm (6 in). Trace the design on to the centre of one of the squares. Do this by laying the fabric over the design and tracing with pencil or, if the fabric is too dense for the design to be read through it, use a transfer pen.

2. Stretch the fabric in an embroidery hoop. With two strands of embroidery thread in your needle, fill in the letters using satin stitch.

3. When the embroidery is complete, press lightly on the reverse.

4. Cut four lengths of braid, each measuring 15 cm (6 in). Pin to the fabric, to form a border all round, trying to ensure that patterns match at the corners. Fold the ends of the lengths of braid under, at an angle of 45 degrees. Stitch in place.

5. Place the embroidered piece on top of the plain piece of fabric, with right sides facing, and stitch all round, 1 cm (1/2 in) from raw edges. Leave a small gap in one of the sides, for turning. Clip curves and trim corners. Turn right sides out.

6. Fill the pillow with wadding and lavender or pot pourri. Tuck in raw edges on opening and slipstitch closed.

7. Stitch lace all around edge, gathering it slightly at each corner as you go.

TEMPLATES: Thank You, page 117

TECHNIQUES: Satin Stitch, page 113

Stitch a small needlepoint pillow with the recipient's initial as a gift.

How to make a needlepoint pillow

You will need

10-count canvas

Tapestry yarns

Tapestry needle

Tapestry frame

Cotton fabric

Polyester wadding

Sewing thread and needle

Tassel braid, to trim

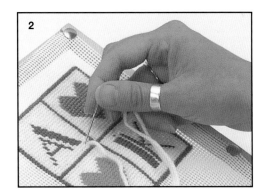

1. Cut a piece of canvas at least 5 cm (2 in) larger all round than you intend your finished cushion to be. Stretch it on a frame.

2. Divide the canvas into squares, with rows of half cross stitch. Following the grid on page 126, fill in the squares with your chosen letters or heart motifs. Stitch the letters and motifs first, then fill in the background.

3. Remove the canvas from the frame. Trim excess canvas to 1.5 cm (1/2 in). Cut a piece of backing fabric the same size. Place the two pieces right sides facing, and stitch all round, close to the edge of the work, leaving a gap for turning. Clip corners and turn right sides out.

4. Make a small cushion from cotton fabric, the same size as the needlepoint cushion. Stuff quite tightly with wadding. Insert it into the needlepoint cover and stitch opening closed.

5. Stitch tassel braid all round the edge of the cushion.

TEMPLATES: Needlepoint Alphabet, page 126

Baby

Whether you have just had a baby of your own and want to announce the news to the world, or you know of a new arrival and want to send a message of congratulation, here are two ideas.

A pretty floral garland, with 'baby' written in French, could be embroidered on a bib, as it has been here, painted on a wooden box, to hold lotions and cotton wool, or toys, or painted in watercolours on textured paper and framed to hang in the nursery. The motif could be reduced in size, or enlarged, or the colours could be changed to shades of blue, for a boy.

For the card, a teddy bear shape is simple but charming. The lettering has been traced from the embroidery motif. You could spell out the baby's name instead, in which case a shorter or longer chain of teddies may have to be cut.

How to make a baby announcement card

You will need

Coloured card

Tracing paper

Pencil

Scissors

Coloured pens or pencils

1. Trace off the teddy bear template from page 116. If you wish, reduce or enlarge it with the help of a photocopier. Cut out the shape to make a pattern.

2. Place the paper pattern at one end of the card and mark off the width. Fold the card at this point. Continue to make folds at the same intervals along the length of the card, forming a concertina.

3. With the card folded, place the paper pattern on top and draw around the outline. Cut out, through all thicknesses, ensuring that you do not cut through the joining points at the end of each paw.

4. Open out your string of teddies and trace letters, or draw them freehand, on to each one. Colour in the letters, using coloured pencils or pens.

How to make an embroidered bib

You will need

White cotton fabric

6-stranded embroidery thread

Lightweight polyester wadding

90 cm (1 yd) of narrow satin or cotton bias binding

1. Trace the motif on to thin paper, including the outline shape of the bib, then trace over the letter on the back of the paper using a transfer pen. Place the design on the fabric and press with a hot iron, to transfer the letter to the fabric.

2. Stretch the fabric in an embroidery hoop. With two strands of embroidery thread in your needle, fill in the letters and flower motif, using satin stitch for wider areas and stem stitch for thin lines.

3. When the embroidery is complete, press lightly on the reverse. Place on top of another

piece of fabric and one layer of wadding. Pin the layers together, and cut out around the bib outline shape.

4. Sandwich the wadding between the two layers of fabric, with the embroidered piece uppermost. Stitch all round, 6 mm (1/4 in) from raw edges, through all thicknesses.

5. Bind the neck edge of the bib with bias binding, then use the remaining bias binding to bind all round the bib, leaving two long ends for tying.

TIPS
Use cotton fabric to back the bib, or terry-towelling for extra absorbency. Towelling can also be used in place of wadding, if you prefer.

TEMPLATE: Bib, Embroidery Motif, page 117
TECHNIQUES: Satin Stitch, page 113

Use simple cutouts to create a card for a new baby or, if you have more time, why not stitch a celebratory bib?

Christmas

Add some festive flair to Christmas with decorative lettering. Start by making your own cards, quite simply, quickly and inexpensively, with letters cut from wrapping paper. Then label stockings with names or initials. Finally, make a Christmas album in which you can store photographs, messages and scraps to preserve your special memories.

The stockings are made using a technique called crazy patchwork, much loved by Victorian needlewomen as a way of utilizing small scraps of fancy fabrics.

The cards are made from letters cut from wrapping paper but if you cannot find a similar alphabet giftwrap, you could photocopy letters from a magazine, or use a computer to generate appropriate lettering.

The projects shown here feature lots of gold, rich fabrics and glitter. But take these ideas as a starting point and choose your own colours and textures to create other Christmas items. Ideas from other pages in the book may provide you with inspiration, particularly the wedding projects on pages 102–105, where the invitations and place cards, the confetti cones and the decorated plates could easily be adapted for the festive season.

You will need

Plain cotton fabric, such as calico

Small pieces of fabric: silk, satin, velvet, brocade

Small lengths of ribbon

Shop-bought alphabet-letter motifs
Crewel needle
Sewing thread
Embroidery threads, including gold thread
Backing fabric, such as velvet or brocade
Lining fabric, such as cotton lawn or silk
50 cm (19 3/4 in) of wide lace

How to make Christmas stockings

1. Cut a stocking shape from calico. You will find the template on page 125. Enlarge this on a photocopier to the desired size.

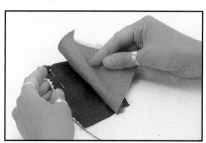

2. Position your first patch on the top left-hand corner and baste in position.

3. Take a second patch and place it, face down, on top of the first, aligning one edge with an edge of the first patch. Stitch a straight seam about 4–5 mm (1/4 in) from raw edges.

Carry on in this way until the background fabric has been completely covered with patches and there are no raw edges, apart from around the perimeter of the stocking shape. Add a few lengths of ribbon, their edges slipstitched in place. Press.

Now add embroidery. Work any fancy stitches you like, such as herringbone or feather stitch, along seam lines. Go over lines of herringbone with a second row, in gold or a contrasting colour. Running stitch can also look effective, particularly when woven in and out with a contrasting thread. Or try couching thick thread or thin cord.

Stitch on alphabet motifs, using a matching coloured thread. Add other embroidered motifs, such as a gold star outlined with backstitch and filled with satin stitch, or a cluster of ribbon roses.

Cut a second stocking shape from a suitably rich fabric, such as brocade or velvet, to a make a back for the stocking. Cut two stocking shapes from lining fabric. To make up the stocking, stitch front to back, with right sides facing, 6 mm (¼ in) from raw edges. Leave top edge open. Clip curves and turn right sides out. Stitch the two pieces of lining together but do not turn. Slip the lining inside the stocking. Turn under raw edges at top of stocking and lining by 1cm (½ in).

Insert the straight edge of the lace between the stocking and the lining. Slipstitch lining to stocking. Add a loop of ribbon to the corner of the stocking, for hanging up.

Let Santa know whose stocking he is filling by adding names or initials in bold lettering.

Use individual letters to decorate gift tags, using the initial letter of the person whose present it is.

Look out for alphabet giftwrap which can be used not only to wrap presents but also to decorate home-made Christmas cards.

You will need

Medium-weight coloured card

Wrapping paper with alphabet motif

Craft knife and steel ruler

Glue stick

How to make simple Christmas cards

1. Measure out and cut rectangles of card measuring 21 x 14.5 cm (8$\frac{1}{4}$ x 5$\frac{3}{4}$ in). Score a line down the centre of each and fold in half.

2. Cut out individual letters from wrapping paper and arrange to spell out a Christmas message. Glue in place using a glue stick.

TIP

You can alter the size and shape of your Christmas cards – but it is a good idea to buy envelopes first and make sure the cards fit inside!

Make a Christmas album filled with photographs, messages, cards and scraps, as a lasting souvenir.

You will need

Ring-bound, hard-covered notebook

Acrylic paint, dark green

Paintbrush

Dimensional paints, red, green and gold

Glitter

Paste jewels or sequins

How to make a Christmas Memory Album

1. Paint the covers of the book with acrylic paint in dark green, or the colour of your choice. Leave to dry.

2. Trace the lettering from page 125. Transfer it on to the centre of the cover.

3. Using dimensional paints, squeezed straight from the tube, go over the outlines of the letters. While the paint is still wet, sprinkle with glitter. Attach sequins or paste jewels with small blobs of dimensional paint.

4. When the paint is dry, tip off the excess glitter.

TIP

Dimensional paint includes a range of different products in gloss, pearl and glitter finishes, for decorating fabrics, china, wood, glass and so on. For this project, almost any kind of dimensional paint will do.

Techniques & templates

*T*he needlework techniques used throughout this book are outlined below, and each is simple enough even for a beginner to attempt. On the following pages, you will find all the designs, in outline or grid form, that you will need to complete any one of the projects, including several basic alphabets.

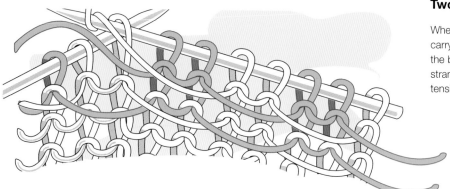

Two-colour knitting

When knitting with more than one colour, carry the colour not in use loosely across the back of your work. Try not to pull these strands too tightly and maintain an even tension throughout.

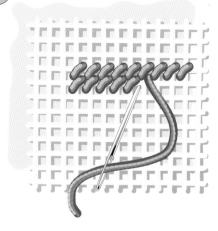

Needlepoint

The little cushion on page 105 is worked in tent stitch, the most common needlepoint stitch. Work it in rows from left to right, bringing your needle up at the top of the stitch and in at the bottom, then from right to left, bringing the needle out at the bottom of each stitch and in at the top. While you are making small, neat, half cross stitches at the front of the work, this method produces longer, oblique stitches at the back of the work, forming a dense, hardwearing fabric.

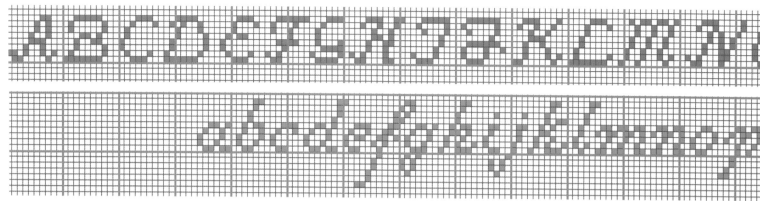

Embroidery

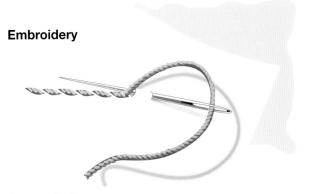

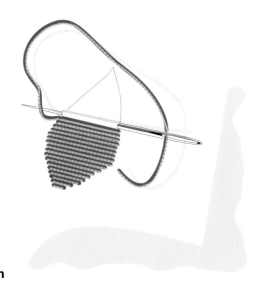

Stem stitch

Use this stitch to make neat lines of embroidery. Starting at the left-hand side of the line you are following, work towards the right, using small stitches of equal length. Push the needle down through the fabric, just below the line and to the right of the previous stitch and bring it up just above the centre of the previous stitch.

Satin stitch

Use satin stitch to fill in solid areas of colour. Bring the needle up through the fabric on the left-hand side of the motif and back down on the right. Work the stitches close together so that no fabric is visible through the stitching. It is advisable to work this stitch with the fabric stretched in an embroidery hoop, to help maintain an even tension.

Cross stitch

Cross stitch is usually worked on even-weave fabrics. Bring the needle up through a hole in the fabric, then across to form a diagonal stitch, then work a second diagonal stitch on top, making a single cross. To work a whole row of cross stitches, first make a row of diagonals, working from left to right for a horizontal row or from top to bottom for a vertical row. Then go back along the row, making crosses. Make sure the top diagonals all lie in the same direction.

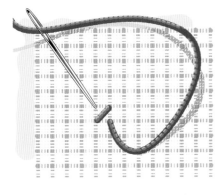

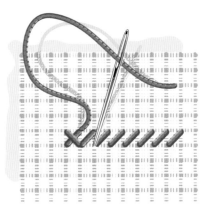

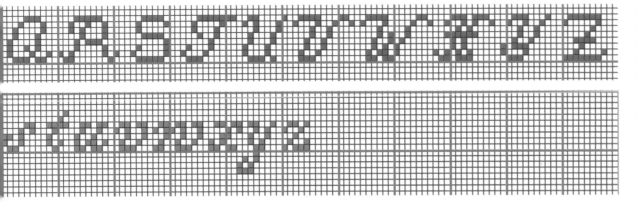

Use these charts to stitch cross-stitch borders for towels and other items. Or rearrange the letters into rows, to make a simple alphabet sampler.

To enlarge or reduce the size of your
chosen template, use a photocopier.
Alternatively, using the background grid
as a guide, copy the outlines onto a grid
of larger or smaller squares.

Martha

Thank you

Bébé

sweet dreams

Enlarge the clock face (left) to
the size you require, to make the
cardboard clock on pages
38–39.

The grid (right), is for the knitted
throw on pages 42–43. Choose
your own selection of letters.
Because space is limited, the
letter 'I' has been omitted from
the chart but can easily be
adapted from the letter 'T'.

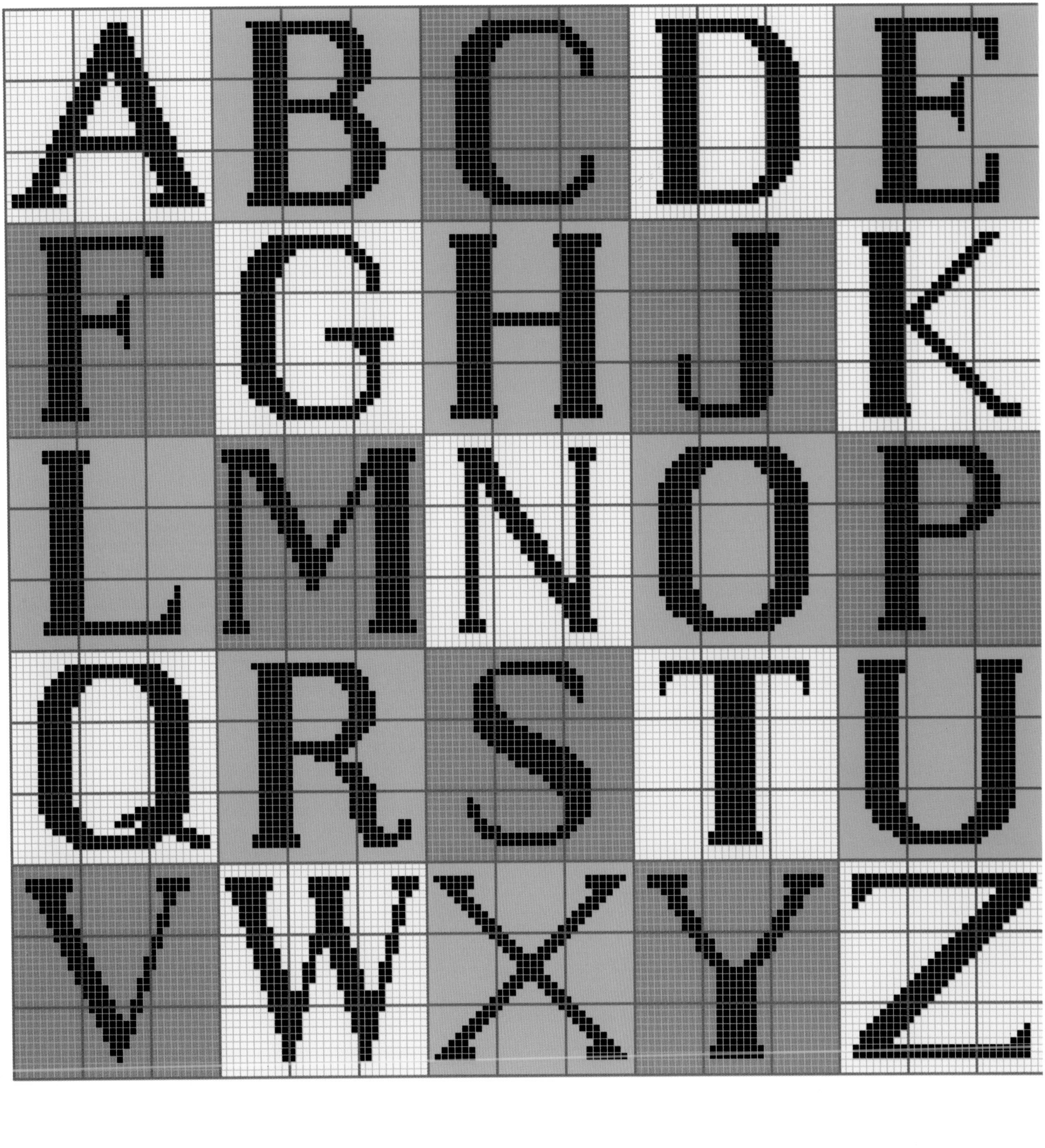

A B C D
E F G H I J
K L M N O P
Q R S T U V
W X Y Z

A B C D

E F G H I J

K L M N O P

Q R S T U V

W X Y Z

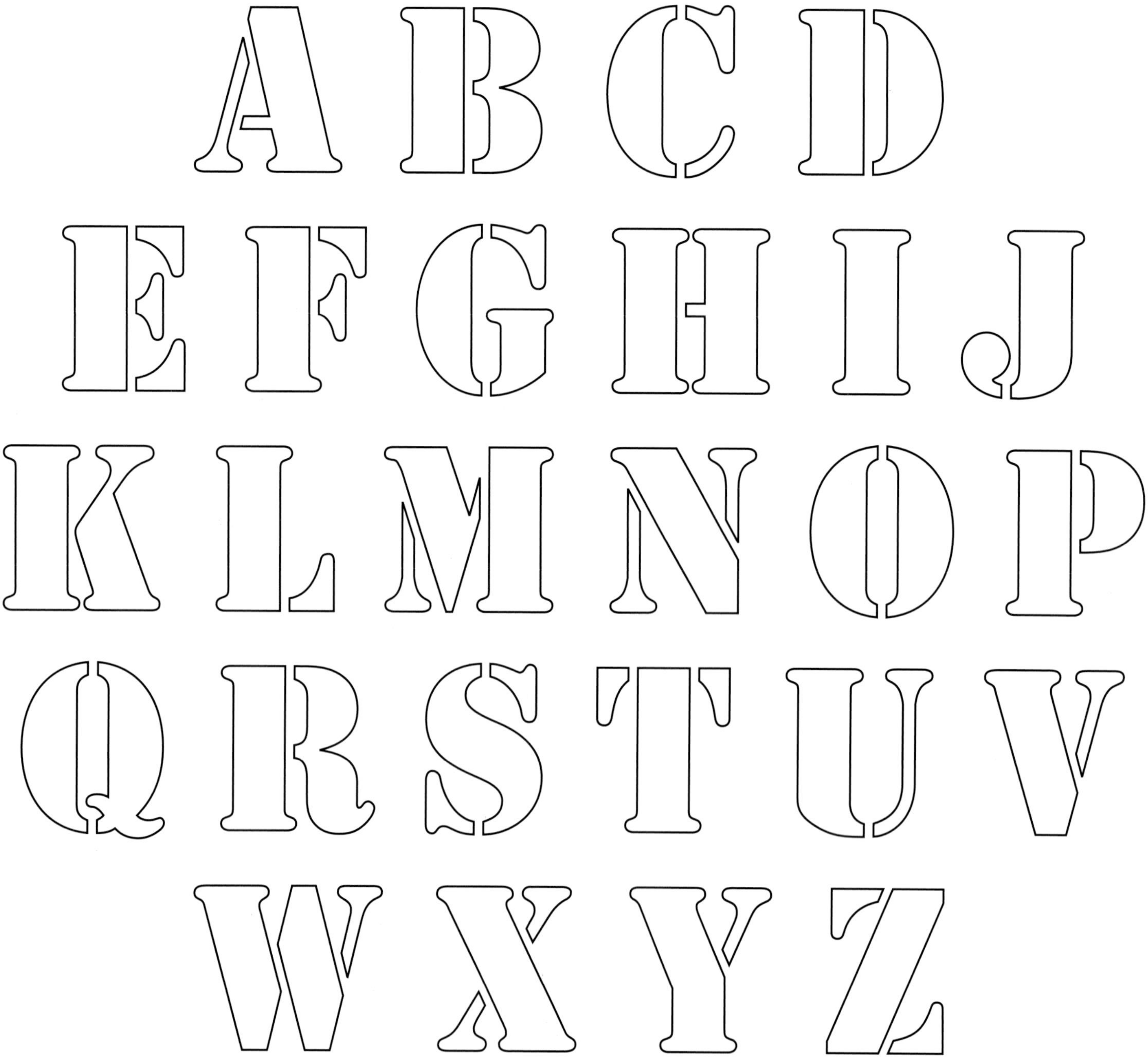

A B C D
E F G H I J
K L M N O P
Q R S T U V
W X Y Z

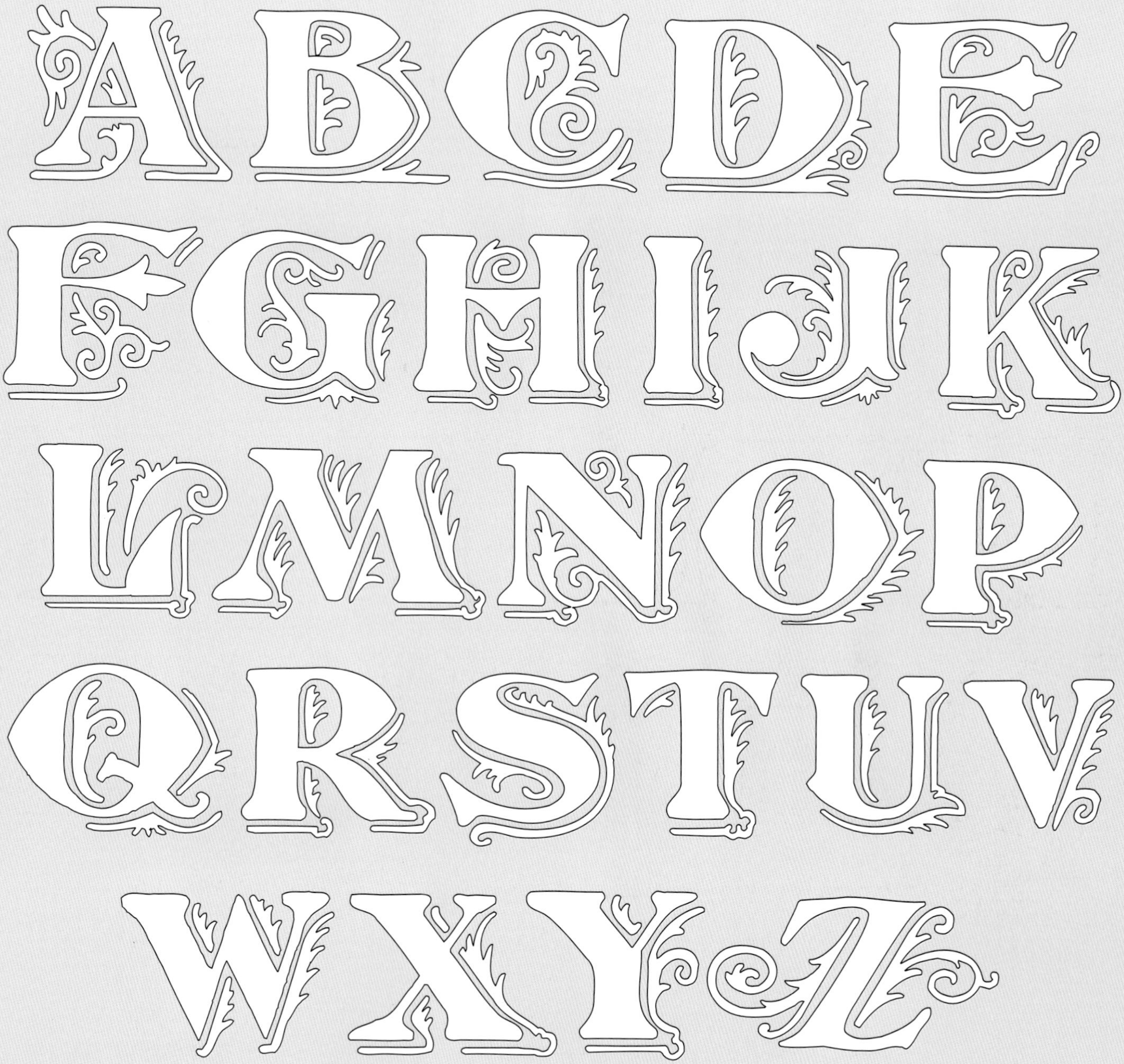

ABCDE
FGHIJK
LMNOP
QRSTUV
WXYZ

Christmas Memories

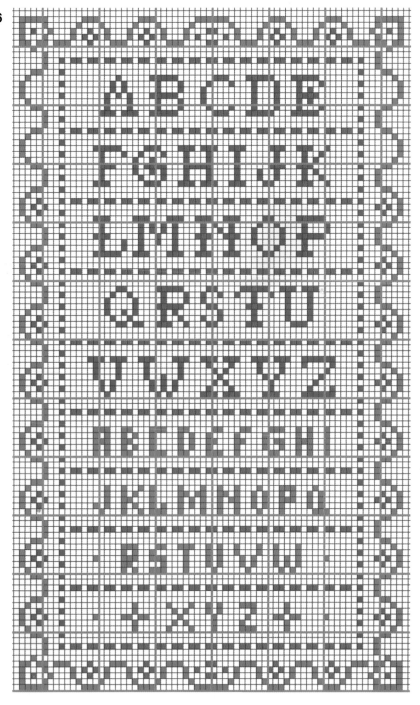

Follow the charts above and on the facing page to make the
cross-stitch samplers featured on pages 68–69. Choose letters
from the chart on the right to stitch a needlepoint cushion like
the one on page 105. Whether you are working in cross stitch or
tent stitch (needlepoint), one block on the chart represents one
stitch on your fabric or canvas.

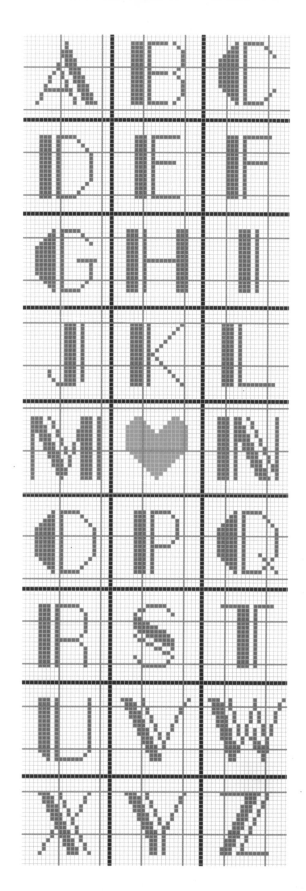

Useful addresses

The publishers would like to thank the following for supplying materials used in making the projects in this book:

Harvey Baker Design
Rogers Industrial Estate
Yalberton Road
Paignton
Devon TQ4 7PJ
MDF furnishing blanks

Coats Crafts UK
PO Box 22
Linfield
McMullen Road
Darlington
Co. Durham DL1 1YQ
Anchor threads, cross-stitch fabrics

Daler-Rowney Ltd
PO Box 10
Bracknell
Berkshire RG12 8ST
Acrylic paints, Canford paper

Decorfin
Royal Sovereign Ltd
7 St Georges Industrial Estate
White Hart Lane,
London N22 5QL
Decorfin fabric and craft paints

Dylon International Ltd.
Worsley Bridge Road
London SE26 5HD
Fabric dyes and paints; Image Maker transfer solution

Offray Ribbon
CM Offray & Son Europe
Roscrea
Co. Tipperary
Ireland
Ribbons

Pebeo
109 Solent Business Centre
Millbrook Road West
Millbrook
Southampton S015 0HW
Pebeo Deco paints, Setacolor fabric paints, Setasilk silk paints and gutta, Cerne Relief, Porcelaine 150

Rowan Yarns
Greenland Mill
Holmfirth
Huddersfield HD7 1RW
Knitting yarns

VV Rouleaux
10 Symons Street
London SW3 2TJ
Ribbons

Scumble Goosie
Lewiston Mill
Toadsmoor Road
Stroud
Gloucestershire GR5 22B
MDF furnishing blanks

Acknowledgements

The author would like to give special thanks to the following people:

Carol Hook, of Clear Communications, for Pebeo craft paints and silk-painting materials. Jon Madeley at Scumble Goosie. Daniel Skillet at Royal Sovereign. Lucy and Christine at Offray Ribbons. Jane Chamberlain at DMC. Emily Readett-Bayley for gilded wooden letters. Kate at Munro & Forster, and Dylon for supplying materials. Mrs Kennedy for stitching the cross-stitch samplers, Tom for cutting out the wooden animals and my mother-in-law, Alice, for making up the waistcoat. The ilustrated alphabet on page 64 has previously appeared in Needlecraft magazine, published by Future Publishing.

Ann Thomson for her creative design and her tireless involvement in the project and Debbie Patterson, whose photographs showed all the projects to their best advantage and who inspired me to make even more items for the book than I had originally intended. Thanks also to Sheila Murphy for, once again, having great confidence in me and being so encouraging, and to Karen Ings for her editing skills and her patience.

My daughters, Edith and Lillie, and husband Tom, for modelling some of the items in the book, and my son Joshua for his help with packing up the items after the photo sessions. And thank you to my father for engendering my interest in typography, to my mother for instilling a sense of style, and to both my parents for encouraging me to be creative.